ACSM Certified Personal Trainer Exam Prep

A concise study guide that highlights the knowledge and skills required to pass the ACSM CPT Exam to become a certified personal trainer.

- Includes quick reference pages for required Formulas, Conversions and Acronyms.

- Includes 50 practice questions to enhance knowledge and to have an idea of what the actual test will look like.

- Includes detailed practice question answers with explanations on how the answers are obtained.

- Includes resources and helpful links that share additional information to help you be fully prepared on test day.

- Includes a link to save **$30 OFF the ACSM CPT Exam**!

- Includes term definitions and detailed descriptions of the heart, muscles, nutrition, training modalities and more!

Visit our website below for additional insights or to message us with any questions you may have while preparing for your exam.

www.cptprep.com
Follow us on social @CPTPrep

Contact via e-mail at info@cptprep.com
Your feedback is welcomed and appreciated!

Copyright © 2018 by CPT Prep

All rights reserved. No part of this publication may be reproduced, distributed, or transmitted in any form or by any means, including photocopying, recording, or other electronic or mechanical methods, without the prior written permission of the publisher, except in the case of brief quotations embodied in critical reviews and certain other noncommercial uses permitted by copyright law.

CPT Prep is not affiliated with or endorsed by any official testing organization. All organizational and test names are trademarks of their respective owners.

This book is intended to supplement, not replace the information provided in *ACSM's Resources for the Personal Trainer (Fifth Edition)*.

Table of Contents

ACSM Certified Personal Trainer Performance Domains 1
ACSM Certified Personal Trainer Test Statistics 1

Domain Breakdown by Chapters in the ACSM Manual 2

Domain I: Initial Client Consultation and Assessment 4
Initial Client Consultation Forms 5
Preparticipation Physical Activity Screening Guidelines 6
Preparticipation Physical Activity Screening 7
Cardiovascular, Metabolic, and/or Renal disease (CMR) 8
Major Signs or Symptoms Suggestive of *(CMR)* 8
Risk Factors 9
Sequence of Assessments 10
Skinfold Measurements 12
One-Repetition Max *(1RM)* Test 13
Posture Assessments 14
Physiological and Psychological Benefits of Regular Exercise 15
Exercise Volume Recommendations 15
Absolute and Relative Contraindications 16
Anatomy and Kinesiology 17
Anatomical Locations and Positions 17
Planes and Axes of Motion 18
Human Movement System 19
Nervous System 19
Skeletal System 21
Articular System *(Joints)* 22
Types of Joints 22
Joint Movement Term Definitions 23
Types of Movements 24
Muscular System 25

Table of Contents

Muscle Proprioception 27
Muscle Imbalances 28
Muscle Action Definitions 29
Muscle Term Definitions 30
Muscle Locations by Area of the Body 31
Muscles of the Core 32
The Heart 33
Methods of Estimating Exercise Intensity 36
Estimating Intensity for Cardiorespiratory Endurance Exercise 37
Ratings of Perceived Exertion *(RPE)* 38
Energy Systems and Energy Pathways 39

Domain II: Exercise Programming and Implementation 40

Components of an Exercise Training Session 41
Muscular Fitness 42
Neuromotor Exercise 43
Skill-Related Fitness Components 43
Biomechanical Principles of Training 44
Force, Torque, and Levers 45
Newton's Laws 46
Calculating Force and Mechanical Advantage of Levers 47
Calculating Work and Power Output 47
Training Principles 48
Acute Variables 50
Resistance Training Modalities 51
Training Recommendations Based on Goals *(Strength, Hypertrophy, Power)* 52
Periodization of Exercise 54
Progression and Regression of Exercises 55
Spotting and Cueing Techniques 56

Table of Contents

General Cardiorespiratory Training Principles 57
Benefits of Cardiorespiratory Fitness 58
FITT-VP Recommendations for Cardiorespiratory Exercise 59
Grouping of Cardiorespiratory Exercise and Activities 60
Physiological Adaptations to Aerobic Conditioning in Untrained Individuals 60
Flexibility 61
Stretching Techniques 62
Designing a Flexibility Program 63
Alignment Issues and Soft Tissue Targets 64
Stability and Mobility 65
Abdominal Bracing and Breathing Techniques 66
Alignment Fault Checklist and Associated Weak or Inhibited Stabilizing Muscles ... 67
Instability *(Balance)* Training 67
Advanced Resistance Training Techniques 68
Plyometric Training 70
Adaptations to Anaerobic Training Programs 72
Speed and Agility Training 73
Programming for Children 75
Programming for Clients with CVD 75
Programming for Older Adults 76
Programming During Pregnancy and Postpartum 77
Programming for Clients with Diabetes 77
Signs and Symptoms of Hyperglycemia and Hypoglycemia 78
Programming for Obese Clients 79
Programming for Clients with Hypertension 80
Programming for Clients with Comorbidities 81

Table of Contents

Domain III: Exercise Leadership and Client Education 82

- Customer Service and Hospitality 83
- Building Rapport 85
- Nonverbal Communication Skills *(Body Language)* 86
- Coaching Techniques 87
- Types of Learners 88
- Types of Feedback 88
- Client Feedback 88
- Behavior Change Strategies 89
- Transtheoretical Model (TTM) 90
- Health Belief Model (HBM) 91
- Theory of Planned Behavior (TPB) 91
- Social Cognitive Theory (SCT) 91
- Goal Setting Theory (GST) 92
- Small Changes Model (SCM) 92
- Socioecological Model (SEM) 92
- Adherence to Exercise 93
- Innovative Strategies to Increase Adherence 94
- Overcoming Barriers 95
- Nutrition and Human Performance 96
- Carbohydrates 97
- Fats 98
- Protein 99
- Fluid and Hydration 100
- Dietary Recommendations Before, During, and After Exercise or Competition 102
- Supplements 103
- Weight Loss 104
- The Female Athlete Triad 105

Table of Contents

Domain IV: Legal and Professional Responsibilities 106

- Business Basics and Planning 107
- Six Basic Business Models 108
- Marketing and Sales 109
- ACSM Certified Personal Trainer Scope of Practice 110
- ACSM Certified Personal Trainer Code of Ethics 111
- Legal Terms and Laws 112
- Risk Management Program 113
- Emergency Procedures 113
- Injury Prevention Program 113
- Musculoskeletal Injury Terms 114

Conversions and Formulas 115

Acronym and Abbreviation Meanings 116

Additional Resources and Helpful Links 118

Practice Questions 119

Practice Question Answers 129

Thank You Page 132

References 133

ACSM Certified Personal Trainer Performance Domains

Domains are listed below with percentage of questions out of the 150 multiple choice questions on the test. You are scored on 120 out of the 150 questions on the test. A passing score is 550 or better out of a possible 800 points. You will have 2.75 hours *(165 minutes)* to take the exam.

Domain I: Initial Client Consultation and Assessment – 25% (37+ Questions)

Domain II: Exercise Programming and Implementation – 45% (67+ Questions)

Domain III: Exercise Leadership and Client Education – 20% (30 Questions)

Domain IV: Legal and Professional Responsibilities – 10% (15 Questions)

The exam questions consist of the following (3) levels of cognitive challenge:

Recall: Remember basic facts, information, or steps in a process.

Application: Comprehend and implement processes, interpret simple results, or summarize information.

Synthesis: Differentiate, relate parts of a system, make judgments on new information based on given criteria, critique a process or product, make recommendations.

ACSM Certified Personal Trainer Test Statistics

2016: 5,389 candidates took the test with a pass rate of 53%
(2,856 passed / 2,533 failed)

2015: 5,226 candidates took the test with a pass rate of 53%
(2,770 passed / 2,456 failed)

2014: 5,152 candidates took the test with a pass rate of 55%
(2,834 passed / 2,318 failed)

There are currently 15,947 ACSM CPT's as of October 25th, 2016.

This study guide was written to help enhance the knowledge required to become an ACSM Certified Personal Trainer (CPT) and to give you the confidence that you are fully prepared come test day! Once you become certified this guide can be used to reference important information as you begin your career as a fitness professional.

Domain Breakdown by Chapters in the ACSM Manual *(Fifth Edition)*

Domain I - Initial Client Consultation and Assessment

Information for this Domain comes from Chapters 3, 5, 10, 11, & 12.

This domain takes you through the process of the initial client consultation and assessment of the client. Preparticipation physical activity screening is the first step where you gather information about your client *(health history, exercise history/status, medical history, PAR-Q)* and then determine their readiness for exercise and the possible need for medical clearance.

Assessments are then performed *(resting heart rate and blood pressure, body composition, posture, etc.)* Physiological assessments are selected based on the needs and goals of the client *(cardiorespiratory, muscular strength/endurance, flexibility)*. The information gathered during the initial consultation, the assessment results, and the goals of the client are then used to help design a program for your client.

Physiological and psychological benefits of regular exercise are covered along with absolute and relative contraindications to exercise.

In this domain, you will also learn about the anatomy of the human body, the study of human movement *(Kinesiology)*, the systems involved with exercise *(movement)*, and their adaptation to exercise. The systems include the Nervous, Muscular, Skeletal, Cardiorespiratory, and Energy systems.

Domain II - Exercise Programming and Implementation

Information for this Domain comes from Chapters 4, 13, 14, 15, 16, 17, 18, 19, & 20.

Program design begins with involving the client in the planning stage of the program. When a client is involved in designing their program, they are more likely to adhere to it and achieve their goals. The program must be safe, aligned with the client's goals, and based on the findings from the comprehensive assessment.

Components of an exercise training session *(warm-up, the conditioning phase, cool-down)* are given as an outline to design specific programs for each client.

Training principles are covered first so that adaptations to exercise are understood. Acute variables *(1) Choice of exercises, 2) Order of exercises, 3) Amount of resistance and number of repetitions, 4) Number of sets, and 5) Duration of rest periods between sets and exercise* are discussed so that programs can be modified as needed.

Training recommendations based on goals *(Cardiorespiratory, Strength, Hypertrophy, Power, Endurance, Flexibility, Balance, Speed, and Agility), resistance training, periodization, plyometric training,* progressions and regressions of exercises, spotting and cueing techniques, stability and mobility training, stretching techniques, abdominal bracing, breathing techniques, and populations with special considerations are all covered in this domain as well.

Domain Breakdown by Chapters in the ACSM Manual *(Fifth Edition)*

Domain III - Exercise Leadership and Client Education

Information for this Domain comes from Chapters 2, 6, 7, 8, & 9.

Customer service and hospitality *(client care)* are the primary responsibilities of every Personal Trainer. This domain begins with building rapport with your client. Rapport begins with the first impression and continues to grow throughout the client-trainer relationship. This foundation of mutual understanding, trust, and respect increases the likelihood of your client's success with their program.

Coaching and communication strategies include the following: *active listening, expressing empathy, motivational interviewing, positive affirmation, intrinsic, and extrinsic motivation.* Types of learners *(auditory, visual, and kinesthetic)* and types of feedback are discussed. Coaching styles and behavior change strategies such as the *Transtheoretical Model (TTM)* can be used to help the client overcome barriers and maintain adherence to exercise.

Teaching client's effective goal setting techniques and types of goals *(SMART, SMALL, process, product, short-term, and long-term)* will help them set challenging but achievable goals for themselves.

Nutritional information and recommendations, fluid and hydration, supplements, and weight loss are also covered in this domain.

Domain IV - Legal and Professional Responsibilities

Information for this Domain comes from Chapters 1, 21, & 22.

This domain is dedicated to being aware of what is within your scope of practice, knowing what your responsibilities are as a personal trainer *(professional and legal),* and the ACSM code of ethics.

Business basics and planning are covered including the six basic business models available for Personal Trainers.

Marketing and Sales are key factors in being a successful fitness professional. Strategies are discussed to give you a blueprint for success in this area.

A risk management program including emergency procedures and injury prevention to mitigate risks is an important responsibility of both fitness facilities and Personal Trainers.

A brief description of common legal terms and laws are given so that you are aware of the requirements. Consulting a lawyer and accountant is recommended to ensure that all legal and business matters are covered.

Domain I: Initial Client Consultation and Assessment

The following areas are covered in this domain:

- Initial Client Consultation Forms
- Subjective and Objective Assessments
- Preparticipation Physical Activity Screening Guidelines
- Cardiovascular, Metabolic, and Renal disease (CMR)
- Major Signs or Symptoms Suggestive of (CMR)
- Risk Factors
- Sequence of Assessments
- Physiological and Psychological Benefits of Regular Exercise
- Absolute and Relative Contraindications
- Anatomy and Kinesiology
- Planes and Axes of Motion
- Nervous, Muscular, and Skeletal systems
- Types of Movements
- The Heart
- Methods of Estimating Exercise Intensity
- Energy Systems and Energy Pathways

Initial Client Consultation Forms

- **Client intake form** is used to obtain critical client contact information.
- **Personal Trainer-Client agreement** sets expectations ensuring a mutual understanding of the agreement and ramifications from the start. The agreement should include the *number of sessions, cost per session, length of sessions, length of the agreement, cancellation policies, refund policies, performance guarantees, and unsupervised training requirements outside of each session.*
- **Health-History Questionnaire (HHQ)**: Medical history, medications & supplements, exercise history, lifestyle information such as nutrition, stress, work, sleep, etc.
- **Exercise history and attitude questionnaire**: Important for developing goals & designing programs.
- **Medical clearance form**: If necessary once preparticipation physical activity screening has been completed.
- **Physical Activity Readiness Questionnaire (PAR-Q)**
- **Informed consent**: Explains the risks and benefits of performing assessments and engaging in a guided exercise program.

Subjective Assessments: Assessments used to obtain information about a client's personal history, as well as their occupation, lifestyle, and medical background. A checklist for gathering information on the initial assessment is listed below.

- Discuss and evaluate the client's prior exercise experience.
- A needs analysis focusing on learning about the client's personal goals and needs.
- The intended time frame for achieving these goals.
- Targeted areas or muscle groups.
- Health issues *(cardiovascular disease, asthma, diabetes, osteoporosis, osteoarthritis, immune system disorders, neurologic disorders),* musculoskeletal limitations, recent surgeries, chronic injuries, sites of pain, and so on.

Objective Assessments: Assessments that address observations that can be directly measured and quantified by the Personal Trainer. Examples of objective assessments are listed below.

- Resting and exercise heart rate
- Resting and exercise blood pressure
- Body weight and height
- Body composition estimates
- Circumference measurements of limbs, hips, and waist
- Calculation of body mass index (BMI)
- Calculation of waist-to-hip ratio
- Measurements of flexibility
- Tests for muscular strength/muscular endurance
- Tests for cardiorespiratory fitness

Preparticipation Physical Activity Screening Guidelines

- Identify those with medical *contraindications (exclusion criteria)* for performing physical activity.
- Identify those who should receive a medical/physical evaluation/exam and clearance prior to performing a physical activity program.
- Identify those who should participate in a medically supervised physical activity program.
- Identify those with other health / medical concerns.

Self-Guided Screening: An individual who is looking to become more physically active fills out a *Physical Activity Readiness Questionnaire (PAR-Q)* without direct input from a fitness professional.

*A sample PAR-Q+ form can be found in Figure 11.1 on Pages 293 - 296 of ACSM's Resources for the Personal Trainer - Fifth Edition.

ePARmed-X+Physician Clearance Follow-Up Questionnaire: A tool that a physician can use to refer individuals to a professionally supervised physical activity program and make recommendations for that program.

*A sample form can be found in Figure 11.2 on Pages 297 & 298 of ACSM's Resources for the Personal Trainer - Fifth Edition.

Professionally Supervised Screening: Involves an individual seeking guidance from a fitness professional to determine their physical readiness for exercise. This may involve collecting a *Health-History Questionnaire (HHQ)* along with a medical examination and clearance *(if warranted)*.

*A sample HHQ form can be found in Figure 11.3 on Pages 300 - 302 of ACSM's Resources for the Personal Trainer - Fifth Edition.

Preparticipation Physical Activity Screening is based on the following (3) factors:

1. The individual's current level of physical activity.
2. Presence of signs, symptoms and/or known cardiovascular, metabolic or renal disease.
3. Desired exercise intensity.

The first step is to determine if the individual **participates in regular exercise** *(30 min of moderate intensity at least 3 days per week for at least 3 months)*. Depending on the answer **"Yes"** or **"No"** the client is then put into that category and screened according to the recommendations below.

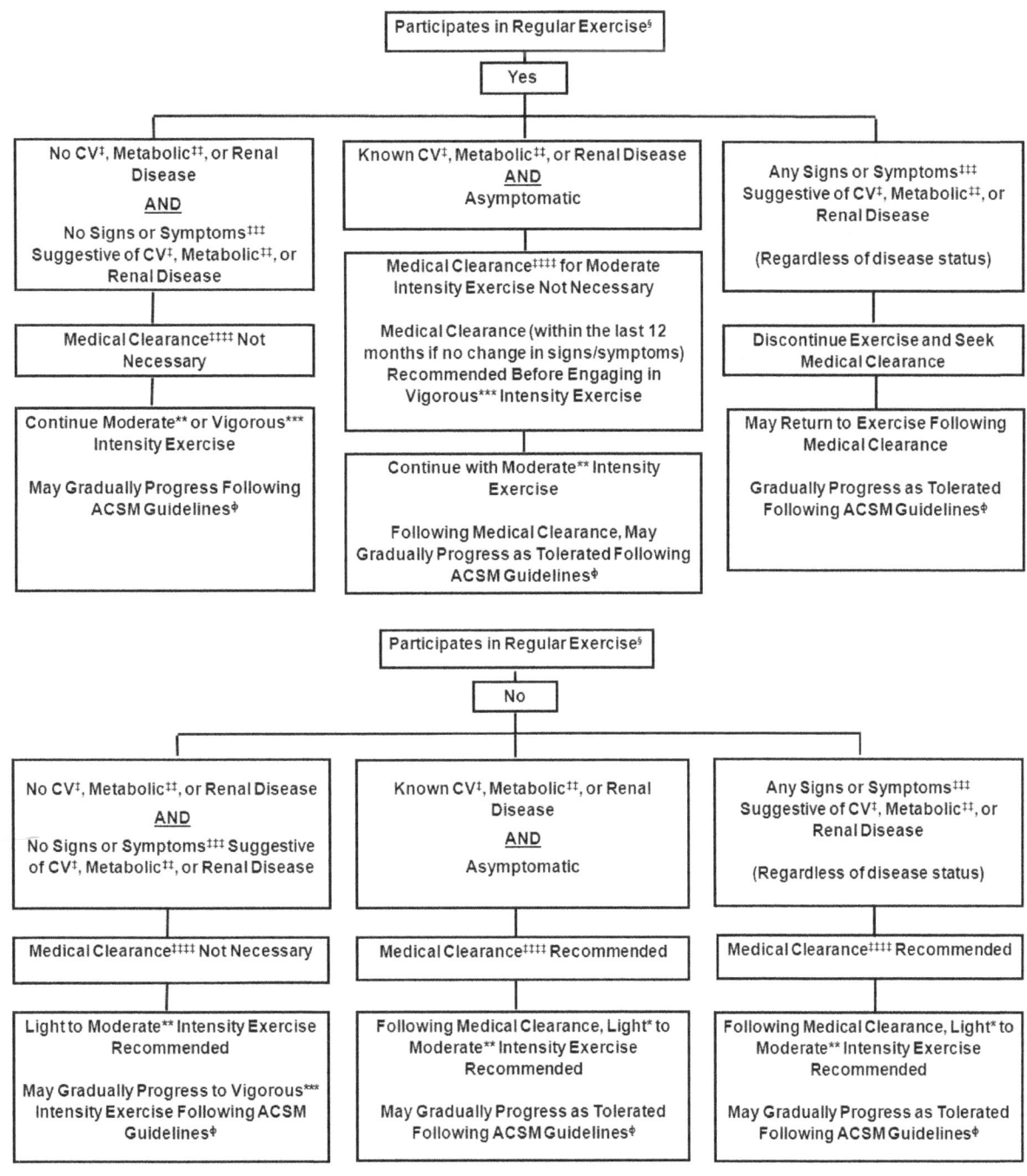

Cardiovascular, Metabolic, and/or Renal disease (CMR)

- Heart attack
- Heart surgery, cardiac catheterization, or coronary angioplasty
- Pacemaker/implantable cardiac defibrillator/rhythm disturbance
- Heart valve disease
- Heart failure
- Heart transplantation
- Congenital heart disease *(congenital refers to birth)*
- Diabetes, Type 1 and 2
- Renal disease such as renal *(kidney)* failure

Major Signs or Symptoms Suggestive of (CMR)

- Pain or discomfort in the chest, neck, jaw, arms, or other areas that may result from ischemia or lack of oxygenated blood flow to the tissue, such as the heart.
- Shortness of breath *(Dyspnea)* at rest or with mild exertion.
- Syncope *(loss of consciousness)*, fainting, and dizziness during exercise may indicate poor blood flow to the brain due to inadequate cardiac output from a number of cardiac disorders.
- Orthopnea refers to trouble breathing while lying down. Paroxysmal nocturnal dyspnea refers to difficulty breathing while asleep. Both are indicative of poor left ventricular function.
- Ankle edema *(swollen ankles)* that is not due to injury is suggestive of heart failure, a blood clot, insufficiency of the veins, or a lymph system blockage.
- Palpitations or tachycardia *(unpleasant awareness of the forceful or rapid beating of the heart)* may be induced by various disorders of cardiac rhythm.
- Intermittent claudication refers to severe calf pain when walking. This pain indicates a lack of oxygenated blood flow to the working muscles similar in origin to chest pain.
- Heart murmurs *(unusual sounds caused by blood flowing through the heart)* may indicate valvular or other cardiovascular disease.
- Unusual fatigue or shortness of breath that occurs during light exertion or normal activity and not during strenuous activity. These may be benign or could indicate the onset of or change in the status of cardiovascular and/or metabolic disease.

*If an individual has any signs or symptoms suggestive of CMR they should obtain medical clearance before beginning an exercise program regardless of their current exercise status.

*A sample preparticipation physical activity screening questionnaire is on Page 303 (Figure 11.5) of ACSM's Resources for the Personal Trainer - Fifth Edition.

Risk Factors

Pay attention to greater than or equal to numbers like fasting glucose. For example, a man who is 45 with a fasting glucose of 100 would be considered to have 2 risk factors.

Age: Men ≥45 years old, women ≥55 years old

Family History: Myocardial infarction *(heart attack)*, coronary revascularization *(bypass surgery or angioplasty)*, or sudden cardiac death before 55 years old in father or other male first-degree relative or before 65 years old in mother or other female first-degree relative.

Cigarette Smoking: Current cigarette smoker or those who quit within the previous 6 months or exposure to secondhand tobacco smoke.

Sedentary Lifestyle: Not participating in at least 30 minutes of moderate intensity physical activity *(40% to <60% VO$_2$R)* on at least 3 days of the week for at least 3 months.

Obesity: BMI *(Body Mass Index)* ≥30 or waist girth >102cm *(40 inches)* for men and >88 cm *(35 inches)* for women

Hypertension: Systolic blood pressure ≥140 mm Hg and/or diastolic ≥90 mm Hg, confirmed by measurements on at least two separate occasions, or on antihypertensive medication.

Dyslipidemia: Low-density lipoprotein cholesterol ≥130 mg or high-density lipoprotein cholesterol <40 mg or on lipid-lowering medication. If total serum cholesterol is all that is available, use ≥200 mg.

Prediabetes: Impaired fasting glucose = fasting plasma glucose ≥100 mg and ≤125 mg or impaired glucose tolerance = 2 h values in oral glucose test ≥140mg and ≤199 mg confirmed by measurements on at least two separate occasions. ***A fasting blood glucose of 126 mg or greater would indicate the individual has diabetes and automatically place them in the high-risk category.***

Negative Risk Factor: High-density lipoprotein (HDL) cholesterol ≥60 mg
****If any other risk factors are present this nullifies or takes one away.***

\> Greater than
≥ Greater than or equal to
< Less than
≤ Less than or equal to

Having one or none of these Risk Factors indicates a low risk of future cardiovascular disease, whereas two or more risk factors indicate an increased risk for disease.

Sequence of Assessments

Initial needs assessments should begin with reviewing a client's health history, completing the intake forms and questionnaires, discussing desires, preferences, general goals and then determining which assessments are relevant and a timeline to conduct them. Periodic reassessments are important to gauge a client's progress towards goal achievement. Adequate time should be given between assessments to allow noticeable changes to develop. The following is a recommended order for performing assessments.

1) **Heart Rate (HR)**: Resting

2) **Blood Pressure (BP)**: Resting
Based on the average of two or more measurements taken during two or more visits.

3) **Body Composition**: Height, Weight, Body Mass Index (BMI), Waist-to-Hip Ratio (WHR), Skinfold measurements *Quarterly body composition assessments are appropriate.*

4) **Cardiorespiratory Fitness (CRF)**: Rockport 1-mile walk test, 1.5-mile run test, Queens College Step Test, and/or the Åstrand-Rhyming Submaximal Cycle Ergometer test. ***CRF test procedures are on Pages 336 – 342 of ACSM's Resources for the Personal Trainer - Fifth Edition.***

5) **Muscular Fitness**: Muscular endurance *(Push-up test, Curl-up test, Body-weight squat test)* Muscular strength *(1-RM testing for bench-press, leg-press & squat, Submaximal strength test)*

6) **Flexibility**: Sit-and-reach test

Personal trainers must always be aware of signs or symptoms that merit immediate test termination when conducting any exercise test involving exertion with their clients and refer them to a qualified healthcare professional if necessary. Signs of serious health issues may not be present until the client exerts themselves. These signs and symptoms include the following:

- Onset of angina, chest pain, or angina-like symptoms
- Significant drop (>10 mmHg) in systolic blood pressure (SBP) despite an increase in exercise intensity
- Excessive rise in blood pressure (BP): SBP reaches >250 mmHg, or diastolic blood pressure (DBP) reaches >115 mmHg
- Excess fatigue, shortness of breath, or wheezing *(does not include heavy breathing due to intense exercise)*
- Signs of poor perfusion: lightheadedness, pallor *(pale skin)*, cyanosis *(bluish coloration, especially around the mouth)*, nausea, or cold and clammy skin
- Increase nervous system symptoms *(e.g., ataxia, dizziness, confusion, or syncope)*
- Leg cramping or claudication
- Client request to stop
- Physical or verbal manifestations of severe fatigue
- Failure of testing equipment

Heart Rate Sites

- Radial *(thumb side of the wrist)*
- Brachial *(anterior side of elbow)*
- Carotid *(neck)*

*Note the carotid artery is not the preferred site due to the possibility of reflexive slowing of the heart rate when pressed. Radial and brachial arteries are the locations of choice.

Body Composition: The relative percentage of body weight that is fat versus fat-free tissue.
* Current body fat targets are 15% for men and 25% for women.
** A certain amount of **essential body fat** is necessary, for men it's between 2 and 5%, and for women it is between 10 and 13%.*

Body Composition Formulas

- **Fat Weight (Mass)** = Body fat % x Scale weight
- **Lean Body Weight (LBW)** = Scale weight – Fat mass
- **Desired Body Weight (DBW)** = Lean body weight ÷ (100% - Desired body fat %)

Height & Weight Conversions

- 1" = 2.54 cm
- 1 m = 100 cm
- 1 Kg = 2.2 pounds

Body Mass Index (BMI): A weight to height ratio. *Weight (Kg) ÷ Height (m^2)*

- **BMI Calculation of a man who is 6ft tall and weighs 180lbs** *(pounds)*

    180 ÷ 2.2 = 81.81 Kg | 6ft x 12 = 72 inches | 72 x 2.54 = 182.88 cm
    182.88 ÷ 100 = 1.83 m | 1.83 m^2 = 3.35 | 81.81 ÷ 3.35 = **24.42 BMI**

Body Mass Index (BMI) Classification		
BMI	Disease Risk	Classification
<18.5	Increased	Underweight
18.6 - 21.99	Low	Acceptable
22 - 24.99	Very low	Acceptable
25 - 29.99	Increased	Overweight
30 - 34.99	High	Obese
35 - 39.99	Very high	Obesity II
>40	Extremely high	Obesity III

*Note: BMI cannot determine actual body composition, which means it can unfairly categorize some individuals (e.g., someone with a lot of muscle mass could be put in "obese" category).

Body Fat Distribution: The location of fat on the body.

Waist to Hip ratio is a good indicator of body fat distribution. Waist ÷ Hip = WHR

Waist to Hip Ratio (WHR)

- Waist circumference ÷ Hip circumference = Waist to Hip ratio
- Health risk is high when above 0.95 for men, and 0.86 for women
- Health risk is high when waist circumference is ≥40" for men, and ≥35" for women
- Low risk is ≤31.5" for men, and ≤27.5" for women

Circumference measurement locations: *Neck, Chest, Waist, Hips, Thighs, Calves, & Biceps*

Skinfold Measurements

- Skinfold locations for men: *Chest, Thigh, and Abdomen*
- Skinfold locations for women: *Triceps, Thigh, and Suprailium*

For a visual of the skinfold measurement locations see (Figure 12.6) on Page 329 of ACSM's Resources for the Personal Trainer - Fifth Edition.

All skinfold measurements should be taken on the right side of the body with the person standing upright. Grasp skinfold by pinching and pulling away from the body with index finger and thumb. Place calipers 1 cm from fingers in the middle of skinfold. Read calipers 1-2 seconds after measurement holding skinfold with opposite hand entire time. Once the skinfold measurements are obtained, use the Jackson and Pollock 3-site Skinfold Formulas to determine body fat percentage. ***See nomogram (Figure 12.7) on page 333 of ACSM's Resources for the Personal Trainer - Fifth Edition.***

Bioelectrical Impedance (BIA) determines the electrical impedance, or opposition to the flow of an electric current through body tissues which can then be used to estimate total body water (TBW), which can be used to estimate fat-free body mass and, by difference with body weight, body fat.

Cardiorespiratory Fitness (CRF): A person's ability to perform large muscle movement over a sustained period; related to the capacity of the heart-lung system to deliver oxygen for sustained energy production *(Also called cardiorespiratory endurance or aerobic fitness).*

Muscular Fitness testing considerations: A good way of expressing muscular strength is as a ratio to total body weight *(relative strength).* **Max weight lifted (lbs) ÷ Body weight (lbs)**

Once the 1RM is determined and relative strength ratio has been calculated see Table 12.7 (for upper body) on Pages 346 - 347 & Table 12.8 (for lower body) on Page 348 of ACSM's Resources for the Personal Trainer - Fifth Edition.

One-Repetition Max (1RM) Test

The one-rep max (1RM) test is used to determine overall upper body strength with the bench press or overall lower body strength with the leg press. 1RM bench press is performed as follows:

1) Warm-up with a light resistance that can be performed easily for 5 - 10 reps at 40% - 60% of perceived maximum.
2) Take a 1-minute rest with light stretching.
3) Perform 3 - 5 reps at 60% - 80% of perceived maximum.
4) The client should be close to the perceived maximum. Add a small amount of weight and attempt a 1RM lift.
5) If the lift is successful allow 3 - 5 minutes of rest before the next attempt.
6) Repeat steps 4 & 5 until the client achieves failure **ideally between 3 - 5 maximal efforts.**

Muscular Endurance Assessment

Push-up test is a common assessment used for muscular endurance. The procedures for the push-up test can be found in Box 12.4 on Page 349 of *ACSM's Resources for the Personal Trainer - Fifth Edition. Normative data of test results can be found in Table 12.9 on the same page 349.*

Flexibility Assessment

Sit-and-Reach test is the most common and most practical to use for flexibility. The procedures for the sit-and-reach test can be found in Box 12.5 on Page 350 of *ACSM's Resources for the Personal Trainer - Fifth Edition. Percentile rankings for men and women can be found in Table 12.10 on page 351.*

Posture Assessments

Posture: The arrangement of the body and its limbs.

Static Posture: The alignment of the body's segments, how the person holds themselves *"statically"* with no movement in space.

Neutral position: The posture of the spine in which the overall internal stresses in the spinal column and muscular effort to hold the posture are minimal.

Dynamic Posture: The position the body is in at any moment during a movement pattern.

Static posture assessments check for proper alignment of the kinetic chain checkpoints, symmetry, and specific postural distortion patterns. Assessment of static neutral posture can be done with a plumb line assessment and a wall test.

*Basic plumb line assessment description (Table 17.4) and Postural corrective suggestions (Table 17.5) are on Page 490 of ACSM's Resources for the Personal Trainer - Fifth Edition.

Progressions for Neutral Posture

- **Stage 1**: Lying on the ground
- **Stage 2**: Seated
- **Stage 3**: Standing
- **Stage 4**: Standing and adding in hip hinging
- **Stage 5**: Farmer carries with bilateral loading
- **Stage 6**: Farmer carries with unilateral loading

Alterations in movement quality can stem from multiple factors including obesity and overweight, sedentary behavior, poor postures, unvaried movement, joint structure, propensity for certain muscles to become inhibited, and age.

The principle of **"Straightening the body before strengthening it"** should be a priority of the personal trainer and client early in a training program. Trainers must work to restore and maintain client's normal joint alignment, joint movement, muscle balance, and muscle function.

*Adding resistance to faulty movement patterns reinforces the compensation and increases the chance of injury. Trainers should ensure their clients have proper movement patterns and sensory awareness before adding resistance to those movements.

Progressive overload is optimized when the following three fundamental features are present: **Sensory acuity (proprioception), optimal stabilization strategies, and mobility.** These features lay the foundation for strength and endurance that is achieved through progressive overload.

Physiological Benefits of Regular Exercise

- Improvement in cardiovascular and respiratory function
- Reduction in coronary artery disease risk factors
- Decreased morbidity and mortality
- Decreased risk of falls
- Increased metabolic rate
- Improvement in bone health
- Weight loss and reduced obesity

Psychological Benefits of Regular Exercise

- Decreased anxiety and depression
- Enhanced feelings of well-being
- Positive effect on stress
- Better cognitive function

Exercise Volume Recommendations

- ACSM recommends participation in at least **_150 minutes of moderate-intensity activity per week_** *(30 minutes per day on at least 5 days of the week)* for weight maintenance and reduction in chronic disease risk.

- Engaging in **_250 – 300 minutes_** of moderate-intensity activity per week can help to **_further assist and maintain weight loss._**

- ACSM recommends **_expending 150 – 400 kcal (calories) in physical activity each day._**

- The recommended volume that is consistently associated with lower rates of cardiovascular disease and premature mortality is **_greater than 500 - 1,000 metabolic equivalents (METs) per week._** *(approximately 1,000 kcal per week of moderate intensity)*

Exercise Physiology is a branch of physiology that deals with the study of how the body responds and adapts to the stress of exercise.

The optimal exercise program should address the following health-related physical fitness components: *Cardiorespiratory fitness, Muscular strength and endurance, Flexibility, Body composition, and Neuromotor fitness.*

Absolute Contraindications

The risks of exercise testing outweigh the potential benefit. The client should not participate in exercise testing until conditions are stabilized or treated.

- Acute myocardial infarction *(heart attack)* within 2 days
- Ongoing unstable angina *(chest pain)*
- Uncontrolled cardiac arrhythmia *(abnormal heart rhythm)* with hemodynamic compromise
- Active endocarditis *(infection of the inner lining of the heart)*
- Symptomatic severe aortic stenosis *(narrowing of the heart's aortic valve)*
- Decompensated heart failure
- Acute pulmonary embolism *(blood clot in the arteries of the lungs)*, pulmonary infarction *(the death of a portion of lung tissue caused by an interruption of its blood supply)*, or deep venous thrombosis *(a blood clot in a deep vein, usually in the legs)*
- Acute myocarditis *(inflammation of the heart)* or pericarditis *(inflammation of the membrane enclosing the heart)*
- Acute aortic dissection *(tear in the inner layer of a blood vessel branching off the heart)*
- Physical disability that precludes safe and adequate testing

Relative Contraindications

The benefits of exercise outweigh the risk. Exercise testing can be done only after careful evaluation of the risk/benefit ratio.

- Known obstructive left main coronary artery stenosis
- Moderate to severe aortic stenosis with uncertain relationship to symptoms
- Tachyarrhythmias with uncontrolled ventricular rates
- Acquired advanced or complete heart block
- Recent stroke or transient ischemia attack
- Mental impairment with limited ability to cooperate
- Resting hypertension with systolic >200 mm Hg or diastolic >110 mm Hg
- Uncorrected metabolic conditions, such as significant anemia, important electrolyte imbalance, and hyperthyroidism

Contraindicated exercises: Movements or positions that are not recommended due to the potential injury risk associated. ***Straight-leg sit-ups, double leg raises, hurdler's stretch, standing bent over toe touch, cervical and lumbar hyperextension, Lat pulldowns with the bar behind the head.***

Anatomy and Kinesiology

Kinesiology is the study of the mechanics of human movement and specifically evaluates muscles, joints, and skeletal structures and their involvement in movement.

- **Biomechanics**: The study of how forces affect a living body. Evaluation of how the body moves.
- Musculoskeletal anatomy
- Neuromuscular physiology

Anatomical position: Standard posture wherein the body stands upright with the arms beside the trunk, the palms face forward, and the head faces forward.

Anatomical Locations and Positions

Anterior: The front of the body, ventral

Posterior: The back of the body, dorsal

Superficial: Located close to or on the body surface

Deep: Below the surface

Proximal: Closer to any reference point

Distal: Farther from any reference point

Superior: Toward the head; higher (cephalic)

Inferior: Away from the head; lower (caudal)

Medial: Toward the midline of the body

Lateral: Away from the midline of the body; to the side

Ipsilateral: Body part located on the same side of the body

Contralateral: Body part located on the opposite side of the body

Unilateral: One side of the body

Bilateral: Both sides of the body

Prone: Lying face down

Supine: Lying face up

Valgus: Distal segment of a joint deviates laterally

Varus: Distal segment of a joint deviates medially

Arm: The region from the shoulder to the elbow

Forearm: The region from the elbow to the wrist

Thigh: The region from the hip to the knee

Leg: The region from the knee to the ankle

A visual representation of the anatomical locations can be found on Page 46 Figure 3.1 of ACSM's Resources for the Personal Trainer - Fifth Edition.

Planes and Axes of Motion

Sagittal plane: Divides the body into the right & left sides. Flexion and extension exercises are primarily involved in this plane. *Squats, bicep curls, triceps pushdown, walking & running are examples of movements in the Sagittal plane.*

Frontal plane: Divides the body into anterior & posterior (front / back) portions. Vertical & lateral movements occur in this plane (abduction, adduction). *Jumping jacks, overhead press, lateral raises, and windmills are examples of movements in the Frontal plane.*

Transverse plane: Divides the body into superior & inferior (top / bottom) portions. Horizontal & rotational movements take place in the transverse plane.
Trunk rotation & swinging a bat are examples of movements in the Transverse plane.

*Note: *The plane in which an exercise occurs is in relation to the body not the position of the body. Performing jumping jacks while standing up and making a snow angel while lying on the ground are both frontal plane movements.*

Medial-lateral axis: Straight line that cuts through the body laterally side to side. In the sagittal plane, rotation happens around this axis. *A hip hinge is a movement that occurs around a medial-lateral axis.*

Anterior-posterior axis: Straight line that cuts through the body from front to back. In the frontal plane, rotation happens around this axis. *Raising an arm laterally is a movement that occurs around an anterior-posterior axis.*

Longitudinal axis: Straight line that cuts through the body from top to bottom. Rotation around a longitudinal axis takes place in the transverse plane. *Spinal rotation with twisting of the trunk is an example of a movement around a longitudinal axis.*

*It helps to visualize the planes and know which movements occur in each. A visual representation of the planes and axes can be found on Page 46 Figure 3.2 of ACSM's Resources for the Personal Trainer - Fifth Edition.

Human Movement System

The Human Movement System is comprised of the following (3) interwoven systems that allow our bodies to move: **Nervous, Muscular, & Skeletal systems.**

Nervous System

The nervous system is a conglomeration of billions of cells specifically designed to provide a communication network within the human body.

Think of the nervous system as the software that tells the hardware of the body when to move, in which direction, and at what speed. ***The nervous system is the conductor and the muscles are the orchestra**

Central Nervous System (CNS): The division of the nervous system comprising the brain and the spinal cord. Its primary function is to coordinate the activity of all parts of the body.

Peripheral Nervous System (PNS): The portion of the nervous system that is outside the brain and spinal cord *(somatic & visceral)*. The primary function is to connect the central nervous system (CNS) to the limbs and organs, serving as a communication relay with the rest of the body.

Autonomic Nervous System (ANS): The part of the nervous system responsible for control of the bodily functions **not consciously directed**, such as breathing, the heartbeat, and digestive processes.

Sympathetic Nervous System (SNS): Part of the autonomic nervous system (ANS) that activates what is often termed the *"fight or flight"* response.

Parasympathetic Nervous System (PNS): Part of the autonomic nervous system (ANS) that stimulates *"rest and digestion"* physiological processes.

*Exercise activates the SNS / *Recovery & rest activates the PNS

Neuron: The functional unit of the nervous system.
*Comprised of (3) main parts: the cell body, an axon, and dendrites.

Afferent neuron: Nerve impulses that move toward the spinal cord and brain from the periphery of the body and are sensory in nature.

Efferent neuron: Motor neurons that send a message for muscles to contract.
*They effect/cause movement.

Mechanoreceptors: Sensory receptors responsible for sensing distortion in body tissues.

Joint receptors: Receptors in and around a joint that respond to pressure, acceleration, and deceleration of the joint.

Proprioception: The cumulative sensory input to the central nervous system from all mechanoreceptors that sense body position and limb movements.

Neuromuscular efficiency: When the neuromuscular system allows agonist, antagonists, and stabilizers to synergistically produce muscle actions in all three planes of motion.

Altered neuromuscular efficiency: Occurs when the kinetic chain is not performing optimally to control the body in all three planes of motion.

Intermuscular coordination: The ability of the neuromuscular system to allow all muscles to work together with proper activation and timing.

Structural efficiency: The structural alignment of the muscular and skeletal systems that allows the body to maintain balance in relation to its center of gravity. *(Optimal Posture)*

Functional efficiency: The ability of the neuromuscular system to perform functional tasks with the least amount of energy, decreasing stress on the body's structure.
*Functional efficiency is a result of structural efficiency.

Motor unit: The functional unit of the neuromuscular system. Consisting of the alpha motor neuron and the muscle fibers that it activates.

Motor output: Response to stimuli that activates movement in organs or muscles.

Motor control: How the central nervous system integrates internal and external sensory information with previous experiences to produce a motor response.

Motor learning: The integration of motor control processes with practice and experience that leads to relatively permanent changes in the body's capacity to produce skilled movements.

Motor development: The change in motor skill behavior over time throughout the lifespan.

Motor behavior: Motor response to internal and external environmental stimuli. The collective study of the previous (3) concepts: ***Motor control, motor learning, & motor development.***

The **neuromuscular junction (NMJ)** is the interface between the nerve and the skeletal muscle fibers.

Acetylcholine acts at the neuromuscular junction to excite the muscle fibers of a motor unit.

Skeletal System

The skeletal system serves the following (5) major roles in the body:

- *Movement*: The skeletal system consists of levers *(bones)* and pivot points *(joints)* the muscular system acts upon to create movement.
- *Support*: Bones are the framework of the body that everything else is built on top of or held within.
- *Protection*: Bones encase vital organs and protect them from trauma. The brain is protected by the skull, the heart & lungs are protected by the rib cage.
- *Blood production*: Blood cells are formed in the bone marrow which is housed in the cavity of certain bones in the body.
- *Mineral storage*: Minerals such as calcium and phosphorus are stored in bones.

Axial Skeleton: Portion of the skeletal system that consists of the bones of the skull, rib cage, and vertebral column. *Composed of 80 bones*

Appendicular Skeleton: Portion of the skeleton that includes the bones that connect to the spinal column including the upper extremities and lower extremities. *Composed of 126 bones*

The bones of the skeletal system are categorized into (5) major categories: Long bones, short bones, flat bones, irregular bones & sesamoid bones. *Bones are living tissues in the body that adapt and become stronger to weight-bearing exercise (increased bone mass, density & strength).*

The epiphysis is the end of the long bone, the primary site for bone growth, involved in red blood cell production. **Diaphysis** is the shaft portion of a long bone.

There are (2) types of bones: Cortical (compact) *more dense* / Trabecular (spongy) *less dense*

A visual representation of the major bones of the body can be found on Page 50 Figure 3.5 of ACSM's Resources for the Personal Trainer - Fifth Edition.

Curves of the spine: Cervical, Thoracic, Lumbar, And Sacral

- *Kyphosis*: Primary curves *(thoracic / sacral)*
- *Lordosis*: Secondary curves *(cervical / lumbar)*
- *Scoliosis*: Lateral deviation of the spine in the frontal plane.
- *Hyperkyphosis or Hyperlordosis*: Deviations of the spine in the sagittal plane

There are **24** individual **vertebrae** in the spine:

- **7** Cervical (Neck)
- **12** Thoracic (Mid-back) *Ribs are connected to these*
- **5** Lumbar (Low-back)

We eat breakfast at 7, lunch at 12 and dinner at 5 is a good way to remember the vertebrae.

Articular System (Joints)

Arthrokinematics: The motions of the joints in the body. *The three major motions are roll, slide, and spin.*

Arthrokinematic dysfunction *(altered joint motion)*: Caused by altered length-tension relationships and force-couple relationships that affect the joints and leads to abnormal joint movement *(arthrokinematics)* and proprioception causing poor movement efficiency.

Hyperextension: Movement that extends the angle of a joint greater than normal

Tendons link muscle to bone / ***Ligaments*** link bone to bone

*Tendons and ligaments have a low blood supply which is why they are slower to heal from injury and take longer to adapt to exercise-induced stresses, compared to muscles.

Types of Joints

Synarthrodial & Amphiarithrodial are non-synovial joints that do not have a joint cavity, connective tissue, or cartilage. *Sutures of the skull *Inferior tibiofibular joint.*

Diarthrodial (Synovial) joints are held together by a joint capsule and ligaments; they are most associated with movement in the body. *They comprise 80% of all joints in the body.*

- **Plane (arthrodial)** joints produce gliding & sliding movements. *Acromioclavicular joint*

- **Hinge (ginglymus)** joints are formed between two or more bones where the bones can only move along one axis to flex or extend. *Elbow flexion and extension.*

- **Ellipsoidal (condyloid)** is a biaxial joint. *Radiocarpal flexion and extension at the wrist.*

- **Saddle (sellar)** Unique joint that permits movements in all planes, including opposition. *Carpometacarpal joint of the thumb.*

- **Ball-and-Socket** is a type of synovial joint where the ball-shaped surface of one bone fits into a cup-like depression of another bone. These joints are capable of moving on multiple axes from the common center of the ball joint.*Hip & Shoulder joint.*

- **Pivot (trochoidal)** Uniaxial joints that permit rotation. *Proximal radioulnar and atlantoaxial joints.*

- **Bicondylar** joints allow movement primarily around one axis with some limited rotation in a second axis. *Knee flexion and extension with limited internal and external rotation.*

*See Figure 3.7 on Page 52 of ACSM's Resources for the Personal Trainer - Fifth Edition for an illustration of a synovial joint.

Joint Movement Term Definitions

Flexion: Movement involving a decrease in joint angle *Towards, closer*
Extension: Movement involving an increase in join angle *Extended, away, further*
Abduction: Movement away from the midline of the body, usually in the frontal plane
Adduction: Movement toward the midline of the body, usually in the frontal plane
Horizontal abduction: Movement away from the midline of the body in the transverse plane
Horizontal adduction: Movement toward the midline of the body in the transverse plane
Internal (medial) rotation: Rotation in the transverse plane toward the midline of the body
External (lateral) rotation: Rotation in the transverse plane away from the midline of the body
Lateral flexion (right or left): Movement away from the midline of the body in the frontal plane
Rotation (right or left): Right or left twist in the transverse plane, usually used to describe neck & trunk movement.

Elevation: Movement of the scapula superiorly (upwards) in the frontal plane
Depression: Movement of the scapula inferiorly (downwards) in the frontal plane
Retraction: Movement of the scapula toward the spine in the frontal plane *Inward, Shoulders move back, chest moves up and out*
Protraction: Movement of the scapula away from the spine in the frontal plane *Outward, Rounded shoulders. *Associated with Kyphosis postural deviation.*
Upward rotation: Superior and lateral movement of the inferior angle of the scapula in the frontal plane
Downward rotation: Inferior and medial movement of the inferior angle of the scapula in the frontal plane
Circumduction: A compound circular movement involving flexion, extension, abduction & adduction, circumscribing a cone shape
Radial deviation: Abduction of the wrist in the frontal plane
Ulnar deviation: Adduction of the wrist in the frontal plane
Opposition: Diagonal movement of the thumb across the palmar surface of the hand to make contact with the fifth digit
Eversion: Abducting the ankle *Feet turn out, *Sole of the foot facing outwards*
Inversion: Adducting the ankle *Feet turn in, *Sole of the foot facing inwards*
Dorsiflexion: Flexing the ankle so that the foot moves anteriorly in the sagittal plane *Foot points up towards the leg.*
Plantarflexion: Extending the ankle so that the foot moves posteriorly in the sagittal plane *Foot points downward like a ballerina*
Pronation (foot/ankle): Combined movements of abduction and eversion resulting in lowering of the medial margin of the foot *Flat footed, *Feet turn out*
Supination (foot/ankle): Combined movements of adduction and inversion resulting in raising the medial margin of the foot. *Bow legged or pigeon-toed, *Feet turn in*

Types of Movements

Open chain movements occur when a distal segment *(hand or foot)* moves in space.
Bicep Curls, Lying triceps extensions, Leg extensions & Leg curls are examples of open chain movements.

Closed chain movements occur when distal segments are fixed in place.
Push-ups, Pull-ups, Squats, Deadlift & Lunges are examples of closed chain movements.

Sagittal plane movements include flexion, extension, hyperextension, dorsiflexion, and plantar flexion joint actions.

Frontal plane movements include the following joint actions: abduction and adduction, lateral flexion at the spine, and eversion and inversion of the foot.

Transverse plane movements include the following joint actions: internal and external rotation, pronation and supination, and horizontal abduction and adduction.

Range of Motion (ROM) is the amount of movement produced by one or more joints.

Center of Gravity (COG) is a point from which the weight of the body may be considered to act.

Base of Support (BOS) refers to the area beneath a person that includes every point of contact they make with the supporting surface. *Feet, hands, or other body parts.*

Effective dynamic movement involves one's ability to control their center of gravity (COG) over their base of support (BOS).

Multijoint movements involve using two or more joints to perform the movement.

Multiplanar movements occur in more than one plane of motion.

Incorporating functional exercises that include both multijoint and multiplanar movements that mimic activities of daily living will set clients up for long-term success.

*Major Joint Motions and Planes of Motion can be found in Table 3.4 on Page 54 of ACSM's Resources for the Personal Trainer - Fifth Edition.

*Major Upper Extremity Joint Movements, Range of Motion, Muscles, and Example Resistance Exercises can be found in Table 3.5 on Pages 60 & 61 of ACSM's Resources for the Personal Trainer - Fifth Edition.

*Major Spine & Lower Extremity Joint Movements, Range of Motion, Muscles, and Example Resistance Exercises can be found in Table 3.6 on Pages 62 & 63 of ACSM's Resources for the Personal Trainer - Fifth Edition.

Muscular System

There are (3) types of muscle: *Skeletal, Cardiac, and Smooth*

Skeletal muscles are consciously controlled. They provide locomotion and stability to the skeletal system. There are more than 600 skeletal muscles in the human body. Approximately 100 are primary movement muscles that are the focus of the personal trainer to help clients achieve increased skeletal muscle activation, coordination, strength, size *(hypertrophy)*, and form during movement patterns.

Muscle fiber types: Type I *(slow-twitch)*, Type IIx *(fast-twitch)*, Type IIa *(intermediate)*
*Type IIa is a hybrid with both fast twitch (explosive) & slow twitch (endurance) capabilities.

Type I characteristics: Red in color, smaller in size, produce less force, slow to fatigue, higher aerobic capacity due to a large number of capillaries, mitochondria, & myoglobin for increased oxygen delivery & usage.

Muscles that act primarily as stabilizers generally contain greater concentrations of Type I *(slow-twitch, endurance)* muscle fibers. The core muscles are an example of this as they stabilize the spine during loading and movement throughout the day. Stabilizer muscles are better suited for endurance-type training *(higher-volume, lower-intensity)*.

Type II characteristics: White in color, larger in size, produce more force, quick to fatigue, higher anaerobic capacity, and decreased oxygen delivery due to fewer capillaries, mitochondria, & myoglobin.

Muscles primarily responsible for joint movement generally contain greater concentrations of Type II *(fast-twitch, explosive)* muscle fibers. These muscles are better suited for strength and power-type training *(higher-intensity, lower-volume)*.

Muscle has the following (4) behavioral properties:

- *Extensibility*: The ability to be stretched or lengthened.
- *Elasticity*: The ability to return to normal or resting length after being stretched.
- *Irritability*: The ability to respond to a stimulus.
- **Ability to develop tension**

Structure of Skeletal Muscle:

- *Epimysium*: The outermost layer of the muscle, made up of connective tissue that lies underneath the fascia and surrounds the muscle.
- *Perimysium*: Connective tissue that wraps around bundles of muscle fibers called fascicles.
- *Endomysium*: The innermost layer of connective tissue that surrounds the individual muscle fibers.

The smallest contractile unit of a muscle fiber *(cell)* is called a **Sarcomere**. Sarcomeres are made up of two types of muscle protein: **Actin** *(thin filament)* & **Myosin** *(thick filament)* which slide across each other to provide muscle contraction *(sliding filament theory)*. The arrangement of myosin and actin gives the skeletal muscle its striated appearance.

Sliding-Filament Theory states that actin filaments at each end of the sarcomere slide inward on myosin filaments, pulling the Z-lines toward the center of the sarcomere and thus shortening the muscle fiber.

Relaxed Muscle Cross Section of a Sarcomere

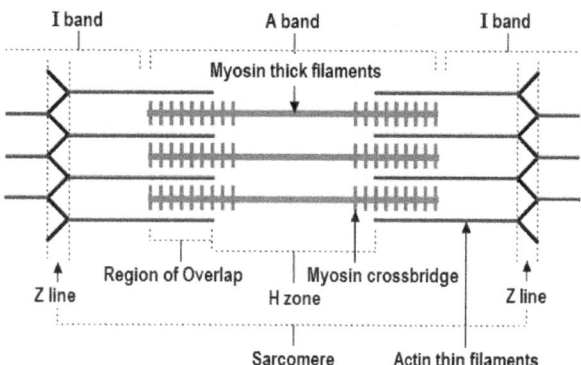

The number of cross bridges that are formed between actin and myosin at any instant in time dictates the force production of a muscle. Muscle force capability is greatest when the muscle is at its resting length due to the increased opportunity for actin-myosin cross bridges. If a muscle is contracted or stretched the force capability is reduced.

See Figure 5.6 on Page 149 of ACSM's Resources for the Personal Trainer - Fifth Edition for a visual representation of the structure of skeletal muscle.

Location and Function of Muscles

Origin: The relatively stationary attachment site where skeletal muscle begins.
Insertion: The relatively mobile attachment site.
Muscle belly: The mid-region in between the origin and insertion.
Line of pull: The direction in which a muscle is pulled.
Parallel muscle: Muscle with fibers that are oriented parallel to that muscle's longitudinal axis.
The rectus abdominis (abs) run parallel to their origin and insertion points.
Pennate muscle: Muscle with fibers that are oriented at an angle to the muscle's longitudinal axis. *Like a feather, it fans out from the origin & insertion. The calf muscle is an example.*
Tendons: Connective tissues that attach muscle to bone and provide an anchor for muscles to produce force.
A **monoarticulate** muscle crosses one joint. A **biarticulate** muscle crosses two joints.

Muscle Proprioception

Proprioceptors are specialized sensory receptors located within joints, muscles, and tendons that provide the central nervous system with information needed to maintain body position and perform complex coordinated movements.

Muscle spindles are proprioceptors that sense any stretching or tension within a muscle; their main function is to respond to the stretch of a muscle and through a reflex action initiate a stronger muscle action *(contraction)* to reduce the stretch, called *"Stretch reflex."*

Golgi tendon organs (GTO) attach to the tendons near the junction of the muscle. They are proprioceptors that detect differences in tension & when excessive tension is detected they send a signal to prevent the muscle from contracting to prevent muscle injury resulting from over-contraction. GTO will signal the muscle to relax after approximately 30 seconds of applied tension to the muscle. *This is why self-myofascial release (SMR) & static stretches should be held for 30 seconds to allow the GTO to inhibit the muscle and allow the joint to be taken further into its range of motion increasing the stretch.*

Muscle spindles (contract) muscles / Golgi tendon organs (relax) muscles

Autogenic inhibition is the process by which neural impulses that sense tension (GTO) are greater than the impulses that cause muscles to contract (muscle spindles), providing an inhibitory effect to the muscle. Activation of a Golgi tendon organ (GTO) inhibits a muscle spindle response, causing the muscle to relax after a stretch is held. An initial static stretch *(low-force)* causes a temporary increase in muscle tension *(low-grade)*. As the stretch is held a **stress-relaxation response** occurs gradually releasing tension.

Reciprocal inhibition: The simultaneous contraction of one muscle and the relaxation of its antagonist to allow movement to take place. The muscles on one side of a joint relax to allow the muscle on the other side to contract appropriately. *Agonist contract / Antagonist relax* *Biceps contract, triceps relax & vice versa.*

Length-Tension relationship (LTR): The resting length of a muscle and the tension the muscle can produce at that resting length. LTR describes the relationship between the contractile proteins *(actin & myosin)* of a sarcomere and their force-generating capacity. When these contractile proteins are ideally aligned with the most cross-bridging, they can produce the greatest amount of force. Shortening or lengthening minimizes the cross-bridges reducing the muscle's ability to produce optimal force. *Visualize a fighter trying to throw a punch into a heavy bag, but they are too close or too far away to land it with optimal force.*

Force-couple relationship: Muscle groups moving together to produce movement around a joint. *Altered force-couple relationships cause synergistic dominance.*

Muscle Imbalances

Musculoskeletal system: The combined, interworking system of all muscles and bones in the body.

Muscle imbalance is the alteration of muscle length surrounding a joint.

Muscle imbalances can be caused in a variety of ways:
- Postural stress
- Emotional duress
- Repetitive movement
- Cumulative trauma
- Poor training technique
- Lack of core strength
- Lack of neuromuscular efficiency

Postural distortion patterns are predictable patterns of muscle imbalances resulting from poor posture, improper movement or injury.

Muscles become dysfunctional when they are either overactive or underactive.

Overactive muscle: Referring to a state of having disrupted neuromuscular recruitment patterns that lead a muscle to be more active during a joint action.

Overactive muscles are shortened, tight, and strong (also called hypertonic).

Underactive muscle: Referring to a state of having disrupted neuromuscular recruitment patterns that lead a muscle to be relatively less active during a joint action.

Underactive muscles are lengthened, inhibited, and weak.

Altered reciprocal inhibition *(altered length-tension)*: Process by which a short muscle, a tight muscle, and/or myofascial adhesions in the muscle cause decreased neural drive of its function antagonist. *Tight hip flexors decrease neural drive to the gluteus maximus inhibiting its function. This causes synergistic dominance where the synergist (hamstrings) takes over to perform the movement.*

Synergistic Dominance *(altered force-couples)*: When synergists take over function for weak or inhibited prime movers. *Understanding and identifying synergistic dominance will help you cue clients into better form.*

Once imbalances are identified, overactive muscles should be lengthened, and underactive muscles strengthened to restore proper length-tension relationships.

Muscle Action Definitions

Concentric: Shortening portion of muscle contraction. *(Moving external resistance)*

Eccentric: Lengthening phase of muscle contraction. *(Control during lengthening portion of movement against force)* *The eccentric action of a muscle "applies the brakes" to slow movement.*

The most effective training programs use concentric-eccentric repetitions.

Isometric: Static, muscle stays in the same place against an external load. *(Joints do not move)*

Isotonic: Same tone throughout a movement.

Isokinetic: Same speed throughout a movement.

Active Muscle Force: Muscle tension that is generated by its contractile elements through the neuromuscular system *(sliding filament theory)*.

Passive Muscle Force: A muscle that is placed in a stretched position creates a passive force that can be utilized during contraction *(stretch-shortening cycle)*.

Concentric activation: The production of an active force when a muscle develops tension while shortening in length. *Concentric means together, toward the center.*

Eccentric activation: The production of an active force when a muscle develops tension while lengthening. *Eccentric activation slows movement, "applying the brakes" to maintain control.*

Isometric activation: The production of an active force when a muscle develops tension while maintaining a constant length.

Isolated function: A muscle's primary function. A muscle action produced at a joint when a muscle is being concentrically activated to produce acceleration of a body segment.

*Learn a muscles concentric muscle action to remember its isolated function. The biceps contract to flex the elbow joint. *Perform the movements to help memorize muscle function.*

Eccentric function: Action of a muscle when it is generating an eccentric contraction. *Incorporating exercises that challenge a muscles eccentric function may help prevent injury during many functional movements.*

Integrated function: The coordination of muscles to produce, reduce, and stabilize forces in multiple planes for efficient and safe movement. *Inclusive of all muscle functions (concentric, isometric, and eccentric).*

Muscle Term Definitions

Agonist: Muscles that work as the prime mover during movement / joint action.
*Biceps are agonist during a bicep curl. *Agonist perform concentric activation.

Antagonist: Muscles that oppose the prime mover during movement / joint action.
*Triceps are antagonist during a bicep curl. *Antagonist perform eccentric activation.

Synergist: Muscles that assist the prime mover during movement / joint action.
*Synergist help the prime movers perform more efficiently.

Stabilizer: Muscles that minimize unwanted movement while the agonist and synergists work to provide movement at the joint. *The core muscles are stabilizers in all movement.

Hypertrophy: Increase in size of muscle fibers

Hyperplasia: Increase in number of muscle fibers

Atrophy: Decrease in muscle fibers

DOMS: Delayed Onset Muscle Soreness

***See the Likert-Type chart to determine muscle soreness in Box 14.1 on Page 380 of ACSM's Resources for the Personal Trainer - Fifth Edition.**

Muscle Locations by Area of the Body

Rotator cuff: Supraspinatus, Infraspinatus, Teres minor, Subscapularis (**SITS**)
- *Supraspinatus*: Abducts the glenohumeral (shoulder) joint
- *Infraspinatus*: Externally rotates the glenohumeral (shoulder) joint
- *Teres minor*: Externally rotates the glenohumeral (shoulder) joint
- *Subscapularis*: Internally rotates the glenohumeral (shoulder) joint

Neck: Levator Scapulae, Sternocleidomastoid, Scalenes, Longus Coli, Longus Capitis

Shoulder / Chest (Anterior): Pectoralis Major & Minor, Anterior Deltoid, Medial Deltoid, Serratus Anterior

Shoulder / Back (Posterior): Upper, Middle, & Lower Trapezius, Rhomboid Major & Minor, Posterior Deltoid, Teres Major

Arms: Biceps Brachii, Triceps Brachii, Brachioradialis, Brachialis

Back: Superficial Erector Spinae (Iliocostalis, Longissimus, Spinalis), Quadratus Lumborum, Multifidus, Latissimus Dorsi

Core (Abdominal): Rectus abdominis, Internal & External Oblique, Transverse Abdominis, Diaphragm

Hip: Adductor Longus, Adductor Magnus (anterior & posterior fibers), Adductor Brevis, Gracilis, Pectineus, Gluteus Medius, Gluteus Minimus, Gluteus Maximus, Piriformis, Tensor Fascia Latae (TFL), Iliacus, Psoas, Sartorius

Hip flexor complex: Iliacus, Psoas, Sartorius, Rectus Femoris, Pectineus, Tensor Fascia Latae

Quadriceps: Vastus Lateralis, Vastus Intermedius, Vastus Medialis, Rectus Femoris

Hamstring complex: Biceps Femoris (long & short heads), Semimembranosus, Semitendinosus

Lower Leg (Anterior/front): Anterior Tibialis, Peroneus Longus

Lower Leg (Posterior/Calf): Posterior Tibialis, Soleus, Gastrocnemius

*Visual representations of the muscles and locations can be found in Chapter 3 - Anatomy & Kinesiology from Pages 69 – 107 of ACSM's Resources for the Personal Trainer - Fifth Edition.

Muscles of the Core		
Local Stabilization System	**Global Stabilization System**	**Movement System**
Transversus abdominis	Quadratus lumborum	Latissimus dorsi
Internal oblique	Psoas major	Hip flexors
Lumbar multifidus	External oblique	Hamstring complex
Pelvic floor muscles	Portions of internal oblique	Quadriceps
Diaphragm	Rectus abdominis	
	Gluteus medius	
	Adductor complex * Adductor magnus * Adductor longus * Adductor brevis * Gracilis * Pectineus	

Local Stabilization System: The local core stabilizers are muscles that attach directly to the vertebrae. They consist of primarily Type 1 *(slow twitch)* muscle fibers with a high density of muscle spindles. Their main function is to provide support and stabilization of the spine. They also aid in proprioception and postural control.

Global Stabilization System: Comprised of muscles that attach from the pelvis to the spine. These muscles provide stability between the pelvis and spine, act to transfer load between the upper and lower extremities, and provide stabilization and eccentric control during functional movements.

Movement System: Comprised of muscles that attach the spine and/or pelvis to the extremities. These muscles are primarily responsible for concentric force production and eccentric deceleration during dynamic movement.

These three muscular systems work together to provide dynamic stabilization and neuromuscular control of the entire core (LPHC).

Lumbo-Pelvic-Hip-Complex (LPHC): Involves the anatomic structures of the lumbar and thoracic spines, the pelvic girdle, and the hip joint.

*These systems should be trained in the proper order starting with Stabilization then progressing to the Global stabilization and Movement systems. A solid foundation of stability must be built in order to move efficiently.

The Heart

There are four chambers of the heart: Right Atrium, Right Ventricle, Left Atrium, and Left Ventricle.

* Think of these chambers as two separate pumps with two champers in each.

* The ventricles "pump" the blood & the atriums "collect" the blood.

The right atrium is responsible for collecting deoxygenated blood coming from the body, and the right ventricle pumps this blood through the lungs. The left atrium collects the oxygenated blood from the lungs, and the left ventricle pumps it to all parts of the body repeating the cycle.

Blood flows through the heart chambers in the following order:
1) **Right Atrium**
2) **Right Ventricle**
3) **Left Atrium**
4) **Left Ventricle**

In addition to the heart chambers, there are also four heart valves that maintain blood flow in a single direction. Blood flows through the valves in the following order:

1) **Tricuspid Valve**: Prevents backflow of blood into the right atrium.
2) **Pulmonic Valve**: Prevents backflow of blood into the right ventricle.
3) **Mitral (Bicuspid) Valve**: Prevents backflow of blood into the left atrium.
4) **Aortic Valve**: Prevents backflow of blood into the left ventricle.

*For a visual representation of the anatomy of the heart see Figure 5.1 on page 135 of ACSM's Resources for the Personal Trainer - Fifth Edition.

The Sinoatrial (SA) node is the pacemaker of the heart. A specialized area of cardiac tissue located in the right atrium of the heart where the electrical impulses which determine the heart rate originate.

The Atrioventricular (AV) node is responsible for delaying the electrical impulses from the SA node for approximately 0.12 seconds between the atria & the ventricles. This allows the right & left atriums to contract & fill with blood. After a brief pause, the electrical impulse moves through the heart bundle branches to contract the right & left ventricles at approximately the same time.

Blood provides the following (3) functions: Transportation, Regulation, and Protection.

Blood vessels are hollow tubes that allow blood to be transported from the heart, throughout the body, and back to the heart, creating a closed circuit. There are (3) major types of blood vessels:

- **Arteries**: Carry blood *away* from the heart. As arteries get further away from the heart, they become smaller and form small terminal branches called arterioles, which end in capillaries
- **Capillaries**: The capillaries are the smallest blood vessels and the site of water and gas exchange between blood and tissues.
- **Veins**: Carry blood toward the heart. Other small vessels, called venules, collect blood from capillaries. The venules progressively merge with other venules to form veins.

Heart Rate (HR)

- Normal resting heart rate is between 60 - 80 BPM *(beats per minute)*.
- The average resting heart rate is 70 - 80 BPM.
- **Bradycardia**: A heart rate that is slower than 60 BPM.
- **Tachycardia**: A heart rate that is faster than 100 BPM.

Resting heart rate (RHR) is the number of contractions of the heart occurring in 1 minute while the body is at rest. *True RHR is measured just before a person gets out of bed in the morning.* Heart rate monitors such as Fitbits can also be worn at night while sleeping to measure an individual's resting heart rate.

RHR is influenced by fitness status, fatigue, body composition, body position, digestion, drugs and medication, alcohol, caffeine, and stress.

__Note__ certain drugs, medications and supplements can directly affect RHR. Clients should abstain from taking non-prescription stimulants or depressants for at least 12 hours prior to measuring their RHR.

A person with a lower resting heart rate may indicate a higher fitness level. An increase in stroke volume as a result of cardiovascular adaptations to exercise reduces the heart rate.

*Higher resting heart rates are indicative of poor physical fitness.

Blood Pressure (BP)

Blood pressure is the result of the amount of blood pumped from the heart *(cardiac output)* and the resistance the flow of blood meets at the vessels. **Blood pressure is defined as the pressure of the circulating blood against the walls of the blood vessels.**

Systolic blood pressure (SBP) is the pressure exerted on the arteries during the contraction phase of the heart *(when the heart beats)*

* SBP increases in a linear fashion with exercise intensity. An SBP that fails to rise or falls with increasing workloads may signal a plateau or decrease in cardiac output (Q).

Diastolic blood pressure (DBP) is the pressure exerted on the arteries during the relaxation phase of the heart *(in between beats)* **Diastolic BP is **determined** when the pulse **fades away.***

* DBP may decrease slightly or remain unchanged with exercise intensity.

The average value of systolic & diastolic blood pressure is 120/80 mm Hg *(measured in millimeters of mercury)*

Hypertension (high blood pressure) is when systolic and/or diastolic blood pressure meets or exceeds 140/90 mm Hg at rest.

Stroke Volume (SV)

Stroke volume is the amount of blood ejected from the left ventricle of the heart in a single contraction. SV is lower in an upright posture *(standing up)* in untrained individuals compared to trained individuals. SV also increases in the supine or prone positions *(lying down)*.

During dynamic exercise, SV increases curvilinearly with intensity. SV reaches near maximal levels approximately at 40% to 50% of maximum aerobic capacity. Once SV reaches its maximum levels, the increase in oxygen demand is met by increasing the heart rate.

Cardiac Output (Q)

Cardiac output measures the overall performance of the heart. It measures the amount of blood pumped by the heart per minute in liters using the following formula:

Heart Rate (HR) x Stroke Volume (SV) = Cardiac Output (Q)

* Cardiac output (Q) increases in a linear fashion with exercise intensity.

Methods of Estimating Exercise Intensity

VO₂ Max (Maximal oxygen consumption): The highest rate of oxygen transport and use that can be achieved at maximal physical exertion. VO₂Max is an indicator of an individual's cardiorespiratory *(aerobic)* endurance capacity.

- **VO₂ Rest**: Resting oxygen consumption (VO₂ Rest = 3.5)
- **VO₂ Reserve**: Oxygen uptake reserve (VO₂ Reserve = VO₂ Max - 3.5)
- **Target VO₂** = VO₂ Max - VO₂ Rest x % of Intensity + VO₂ Rest

Fitness categories for maximal aerobic power for men and women by age are found in Table 15.3 on Pages 425 - 430 of ACSM's Resources for the Personal Trainer - Fifth Edition.

The recommended range of intensity for **Target VO₂ is 40% - 89%** depending on the individual's current fitness level. The Personal Trainer should make adjustments to workload based on the client's response to the exercise load.

Metabolic Equivalent (MET): An index of energy expenditure. One MET is the rate of energy expenditure while at rest that is equal to an oxygen uptake (VO₂) of 3.5.

- MET = VO₂ ÷ 3.5
- Calories expended per minute = (MET x 3.5 x Body Weight in Kg) ÷ 200

Metabolic calculations for various activities are in Box 15.2 on Page 421 & examples are in Box 15.3 on Pages 422 - 424 of ACSM's Resources for the Personal Trainer - Fifth Edition.

Approximate MET energy requirements for various cardiorespiratory training are in Tables 15.4 - 15.8 from Pages 431 - 433 of ACSM's Resources for the Personal Trainer - Fifth Edition.

Ventilatory Threshold is the point of transition between predominately aerobic energy production to anaerobic energy production. With regular exercise, a person's ventilatory or lactate threshold can increase for some time beyond their primary increase in VO₂ Max. The **first ventilatory threshold (VT1)** or *"crossover"* point represents a level of intensity at which blood lactate accumulates faster than it can be cleared, which causes the person to breathe faster in an effort to blow off the extra CO₂ produced. The *"talk test" (if a person can talk comfortably in sentences while performing the exercise)* is a good indicator that someone is training below VT1. The **second ventilatory threshold (VT2)** occurs at the point of intensity where blowing off the CO₂ is no longer adequate to buffer the rapidly increasing lactate. High-intensity exercise *(≥VT2)* can only be sustained for a brief period due to the accumulation of lactate. A person's heart rate can be determined at both VT1 and VT2 thresholds by using the Submaximal talk test for VT1 and VT2 threshold testing.

VT1 & VT2 metabolic markers can be used to divide training intensity into the following 3 zones.

- **Zone 1** *(low to moderate exercise)* reflects heart rates below VT1.
- **Zone 2** *(moderate to vigorous exercise)* reflects heart rates above VT1 to just below VT2.
- **Zone 3** *(vigorous to very vigorous exercise)* reflects heart rates at or above VT2.

Heart Rate and Heart Rate Reserve (HRR)

Max Heart Rate (HR_{max}): The maximum number of beats per minute (BPM).

- HR_{max} = 220 – Age | A 30 year old would have HR_{max} of 190 BPM | 220 – 30 = 190 BPM
- Recommended range of intensity for *Target HR is 64% - 76% and up to 95% of HR_{max}.*
- The total range would be 122 – 180 beats per minute (BPM) for a 30-year-old.
- *For apparently healthy individuals the range is often narrowed to 70% - 85% of HR_{max}.*
- *Very deconditioned clients would start at a lower intensity of 55% - 70% of HR_{max}.*

*See Table 15.9 on Page 435 of ACSM's Resources for the Personal Trainer - Fifth Edition for other commonly used equations for estimating maximal heart rate. When estimating a client's HR_{max}, choose an equation that most represents the client population.

Heart Rate Reserve (HRR): The difference between max heart rate and resting heart rate.

- HRR = HR_{max} – HR_{rest} | 30 year old with a resting HR of 60 BPM | 190 - 60 = 130 BPM

Target Heart Rate (THR) = HRR x % Intensity + HR_{rest} **(Karvonen method)**

- 30 year old above to train at 80% intensity | 130 x 0.80 + 60 = 164 BPM (THR)
- Recommended range of intensity using the Karvonen method for **HRR is 40% - 85%.**
- The total range would be 112 – 171 beats per minute (BPM) for the 30-year-old above.
- *A range of 60% - 80% may be appropriate for a moderately active client.*
- *A range of 40% - 50% may be more appropriate for a deconditioned client.*

Estimating Intensity for Cardiorespiratory Endurance Exercise								
Intensity	Relative Intensity			RPE (6-20)	Intensity (% VO_{2Max}) Relative to Maximal Exercise Capacity in MET			Absolute Intensity (METs)
	% HRR (VO_2R)	% HR_{Max}	% VO_{2Max}		20 MET	10 MET	5MET	
Very Low	≤ 30	≤ 57	≤ 37	≤ 9	≤ 34	≤ 37	≤ 44	≤ 2
Low	30–39	57–63	37–45	9–11	34–42	37–45	44–51	2.0–2.9
Moderate	40–59	64–76	46–63	12–13	43–61	46–63	52–67	3.0–5.9
Vigorous	60–89	77–95	64–90	14–17	62–90	64–90	68–91	6.0–8.7
Near max to Maximal	≥ 90	≥ 96	≥ 91	≥ 18	≥ 91	≥ 91	≥ 92	≥ 8.8

*Intensity ranges should be selected based on the client's fitness level, health status, & goals.

Ratings of Perceived Exertion (RPE): A method for individual's to subjectively rate overall feelings of exertion during exercise. See the 6-20 point *(classic scale)* below.

Ratings of Perceived Exertion (RPE)	
6	No exertion at all
7	Extremely light
8	
9	Very light
10	
11	Light
12	
13	Somewhat hard
14	
15	Hard (heavy)
16	
17	Very hard
18	
19	Extremely hard
20	Maximal exertion

*RPE is commonly used to determine exercise intensity for older adults or those who are taking medications such as Beta-blockers which influence the heart rate (HR).

Energy Systems

Adenosine triphosphate (ATP) is a high-energy compound required to do all mechanical work produced by the human body.

Muscle fibers produce ATP by three pathways: *Creatine phosphate (CP), Anaerobic Glycolysis & Aerobic Oxidation.*

Anaerobic energy systems do not require oxygen to produce energy. They are the immediate short-term systems used in the first few minutes of exercise. ATP stored in muscle, Creatine Phosphate (PCr) & Anaerobic Glycolysis make up the anaerobic energy systems.
*Strength & Power training primarily use anaerobic pathways (ATP-PC & Anaerobic Glycolysis)

The Aerobic system requires oxygen to produce energy. It uses carbohydrates, fats & proteins to produce ATP. Carbohydrates are the primary source of energy at the onset of exercise & during high-intensity work followed by fats during prolonged exercise of low to moderate intensity *(longer than 30 minutes)* & then proteins.
*Endurance training primarily uses aerobic pathways (Aerobic Oxidation, The Oxidative System)

Performance of every sport or activity uses a percentage of all three energy systems. The magnitude of the contribution of each system is primarily dependent on the intensity and duration of the activity being performed. **At no time, during either exercise or rest, does any single energy system provide the complete supply of energy.*

Oxygen deficit refers to the lag of oxygen consumption at the beginning of exercise. Oxygen consumption builds gradually at the onset of exercise causing the body to supply part of the ATP required through anaerobic metabolism. Once *"steady state"* aerobic exercise is reached all of the ATP is supplied from aerobic oxidation.

Excess Postexercise Oxygen Consumption (EPOC): Refers to the consumption of more than usual amounts of oxygen after exercise. Oxygen uptake remains elevated above resting levels for several minutes during recovery from exercise. EPOC helps to restore your body to its normal, resting level of metabolic function *(called homeostasis)* by replenishing creatine phosphate (CP) in muscles and oxygen in blood and tissues.

Energy Pathways

ATP: 0-4 Seconds (Strength & Power)*Uses ATP stored in muscles

ATP+PCr: 0-10 seconds (Sustained Power)

ATP+PCr+Lactic Acid: 0-90 seconds (Anaerobic Power-Endurance)

Aerobic Oxidation: 90 seconds to 3+ minutes (Aerobic Endurance)

*For a visual representation & types of performance associated with these energy pathways see Figure 5.4 on Page 145 of ACSM's Resources for the Personal Trainer - Fifth Edition.

Domain II: Exercise Programming and Implementation

The following areas are covered in this domain:

- Components of an Exercise Training Session
- Exercise selection and programming factors
- Muscular Fitness
- Neuromotor Exercise
- Skill Related Fitness Components
- Biomechanical Principles of Training
- Force, Torque, and Levers
- Calculating Force and Mechanical Advantage of Levers
- Training Principles
- Resistance Training Modalities
- Acute Variables
- Training Recommendations Based on Goals
- Periodization of Exercise
- Progression and Regression of Exercises
- Spotting and Cueing Techniques
- General Cardiorespiratory Training Principles
- Flexibility and Stretching Techniques
- Designing Flexibility Programs
- Stability and Mobility
- Abdominal Bracing and Breathing Techniques
- Alignment Fault Checklist and Associated Weak or Inhibited Stabilizing Muscles
- Instability (Balance) Training
- Advanced Resistance Training Techniques
- Plyometric Training
- Adaptations to Anaerobic Training Programs
- Speed and Agility Training
- Programming for Special Populations

Components of an Exercise Training Session

Warm-up: At least 5-10 minutes of low to moderate cardiorespiratory and muscular endurance activities. The goal of the warm-up is to prepare the body for the upcoming workout.
Dynamic stretching, Bodyweight movements, elliptical, treadmill or other cardio equipment.

Conditioning: At least 20-60 minutes of aerobic, resistance, neuromotor, and/or sports specific activities. The goal is to provide an appropriate overload to promote beneficial adaptations.
Exercise bouts of 10 minutes are acceptable if the individual accumulates at least 20-60 minutes total.

Cool-down: At least 5-10 minutes of low to moderate cardiorespiratory and muscular endurance activities. The cool-down transitions the systems of the body back to resting levels.
Stretching, Bodyweight movements, decompressing from the workout.

Flexibility: At least 10 minutes of stretching exercise performed after the warm-up or cool-down phases. *Static stretches should be avoided before resistance training. Dynamic stretches can be done prior to resistance training.*

Exercise selection and programming factors to consider include the following:

- Client's goals and attitude
- Client's fitness and skill level
- Any musculoskeletal issues or injuries
- Any recommendations from the client's health care providers
- Considerations on the particular training day *(client is tired, sore, has been ill, has not trained regularly)*
- Availability of equipment and other activities occurring within the fitness center.

Session components can include some or all of the following:

- Greeting
- Appropriate warm-up
- Cardiorespiratory aerobic or anaerobic interval work
- Cool-down phase
- Muscular strength/endurance component: Traditional and functional exercises
- Core work for stability
- Condition-specific exercises *(orthopedic protocols, pregnancy protocol)*
- Neuromotor training *(promotion of balance, agility, and coordination)*
- Flexibility component
- Goal setting and farewell
- Charting

Table 18.1 on Page 511 of ACSM's Resources for the Personal Trainer - Fifth Edition shows a checklist for each of these personal training session components.

Muscular Fitness

Muscular fitness refers to both muscular strength and muscular endurance.

Muscular strength: The ability of a muscle or muscle group to exert force *(usually measured by one-repetition maximum 1RM)*.

Muscular endurance: The ability of a muscle or muscle group to continually perform without fatigue *(measured by repeated or sustained muscle contractions)*.

- **Frequency**: Varies depending on the goals of the client. For general muscular fitness, 2-3 days per week of full body resistance training is recommended *(chest, shoulders, back, abdomen, hips, and legs)*. At least 48 hours should separate workouts targeting any given muscle group to allow time for adaptations to occur.

- **Intensity**: Typically 8 - 12 repetitions per set at an intensity of between 60% - 80% of the individuals one repetition max (1RM). Older and very deconditioned individuals should initially start with a lower intensity *(10 - 20 reps at 40% - 50% of 1RM)*. Intensity is inversely related to the number of repetitions performed **(Higher resistance = Fewer repetitions).** *To lower the chance of injury and extreme muscle soreness, the number of repetitions selected should allow for muscle fatigue at the end of the set but not failure.*

- **Time**: For adults, each muscle group should be trained with 2 - 4 sets with rest intervals of 2 - 3 minutes between sets. *The total time spent will vary depending on the program (split-routine, whole-body approach).*

- **Type**: Free weights, machines, rubber bands/cords, and body weight. *Opposing muscle groups (agonists / antagonists) should be included when selecting exercises in order to prevent muscle imbalances.*

- **Volume**: 2 - 4 sets per muscle group. These can be the same exercise or combination of exercises affecting the same muscle group.

- **Progression**: Progressive overload can be done in various ways by increasing the amount of resistance lifted, number of repetitions, number of sets, or number of days per week the muscle groups are trained.

Sample resistance training progressions can be found in Table 13.2 on Page 362 of ACSM's Resources for the Personal Trainer - Fifth Edition.

Examples of resistance training exercises for major body areas can be found in Table 13.3 on Page 364 of ACSM's Resources for the Personal Trainer - Fifth Edition.

Neuromotor Exercise

Involves the following motor skills: *Balance, Coordination, Agility, and Proprioceptive training.*
*These activities are also referred to as Functional Fitness or Movement.

- **Frequency**: At least 2 - 3 days per week for 20 - 30 minutes in duration.
  *Programs can range from 1 – 7 days per week.
- **Intensity**: Balance training intensity can be manipulated by the following 3 aspects:
  1) Base of support *(narrowing the base of support will increase the challenge)*
  2) Center of mass *(displacing the center of mass increases difficulty)*
  3) Peripheral cues *(visual, vestibular (eyes closed), and proprioceptive pathways)*
- **Time**: Improvements have been noted with 20 - 30 minutes or more per day for a total of 60 minutes per week.
- **Type**: See Table 13.5 on Page 367 of *ACSM's Resources for the Personal Trainer - Fifth Edition* for a sample progressive balance program. Other various activities can also be used such as Yoga, Pilates, Jiu Jitsu, and Tai chi.

*See Table 13.4 on Page 366 of ACSM's Resources for the Personal Trainer - Fifth Edition for factors affecting the intensity of balance training.

Advanced Training Options

Advanced training options can increase the challenge of an exercise program by manipulating current exercises through the FITT-VP principles. Prescribing new or additional exercises that focus on the skill-related components of physical fitness can also increase the challenge.

Skill-Related Fitness Components

- **Speed**: The ability to perform a movement within a short amount of time.
- **Agility**: The ability to change the position of the body in space with speed and accuracy.
- **Coordination**: The ability to use the senses together with the body parts while performing tasks smoothly and accurately.
- **Balance**: The maintenance of equilibrium while stationary or moving.
- **Power**: The rate at which one can perform work. ***Power = Work ÷ Time***
- **Reaction time**: The time elapsed between stimulation and the beginning of the response.

There are several types of advanced training options to target these skill related components simultaneously. Options such as *high-intensity interval training (HIIT), high-velocity weight training, Olympic weight lifting, plyometric training, balance training, sport-specific, and nonsport-specific agility, and coordination drills.*

*See Table 13.9 on Page 371 of ACSM's Resources for the Personal Trainer - Fifth Edition for examples of activities involving the skill-related components of fitness.

Biomechanical Principles of Training

Biomechanics focuses on the mechanisms through which the musculoskeletal components interact to create movement.

Strength is the ability to exert force.

Work is the product of the force exerted on an object and the distance the object moves in the direction in which the force is exerted.

- *Work = Force x Displacement*
- *Work = Torque x Angular Displacement*

Power is the time rate of doing work *(explosive strength)*

- *Power = Work ÷ Time*
- *Power = Force x Velocity*

Although the word **strength** is often associated with slow speeds and the word **power** with high velocities of movement, both variables reflect the ability to exert force at a given velocity. Power is a direct mathematical function of force and velocity.

The sport of weightlifting *(Olympic lifting)* has a much higher power component than the sport of powerlifting, due to the higher movement velocities with heavy weights of the weightlifting (Olympic style) movements.

International System of Units (SI)

- Force is measured in newtons (N)
- Distance is measured in meters (m)
- Work is measured in joules (J)
- Time is measured in seconds (s)
- Power is measured in watts (W)

1 pound (lb) = 4.45 newtons (N)

Mechanical measures quantify the effort in terms of forces created during the training bout.

Metabolic measures are related to the amount of nutritional energy required to complete the exercise.

Force, Torque, and Levers

Force: A push or pull that can create, stop, or change movement. **Force = Mass x Acceleration**

Muscle Force: Force generated by biochemical activity, or the stretching of noncontractile tissues, that tends to draw the opposite ends of a muscle toward each other.

Resistive Force: Force generated by a source external to the body that acts contrary to the muscle force.

Torque: The degree to which a force tends to rotate an object about a specified fulcrum.

Fulcrum: The pivot point of a lever.

Lever: A relatively rigid rod or bar that rotates around a fulcrum *(pivot point)*. There are (3) different types of lever classes where an effort or force and a resistance are applied.

- **First-class lever**: A lever for which the muscle force and resistive force act on opposite sides of the fulcrum. *A playground seesaw with someone on each end. A neck extension is an example in the human body. (think agonist & antagonist muscles on opposite side of a joint)*

- **Second-class lever**: The fulcrum is toward the end of one side *(either side)*. Both the applied force and the resistance are on the same side with the resistance closer to the fulcrum *(pivot point)*. *Moving a loaded wheelbarrow is an example. *A calf raise is an example for the human body. The ball of the foot is the fulcrum, the weight of the body is the resistance, and the calf muscle applies the force.*

- **Third-class lever**: The fulcrum is toward the end of one side *(either side)*. Both the applied force and the resistance are on the same side with the applied force closer to the fulcrum *(pivot point)*. *Using a shovel to scoop up gravel is an example. The top hand is the fulcrum as the other hand applies the force to pick up the gravel (resistance). *A dumbbell biceps curl is an example of a third-class lever in the human body.*

For a visual representation of the examples above see Figure 4.2 on Page 114 of ACSM's Resources for the Personal Trainer - Fifth Edition.

Moment Arm: The perpendicular distance from the line of action of the force to the fulcrum.

Mechanical advantage: The ratio of a moment *(force)* arm through which an applied force acts to that through which a resistive force acts.

The magnitude of a load being lifted is not equal to the load placed on the body.
Most of the skeletal muscles operate at a considerable mechanical disadvantage due to the lever arrangement within the body relative to the external forces the body resists. Forces in the muscles and tendons are much higher than those exerted by the hands or feet on external objects or the ground.

Newton's (3) Laws of Linear Motion

1) **Law of Inertia**: An object at rest stays at rest, and an object in motion stays in motion with the same speed and in the same direction *(velocity)* unless acted on by an external force.

2) **Law of Acceleration**: The linear acceleration of an object is produced by a force directly proportional to that force and inversely proportional to the object's mass.
   Force = Mass x Acceleration

3) **Law of Reaction**: For every force, there is a reaction force equal in magnitude and opposite in direction.

Newton's (3) Laws of Angular Movement

1) *Law of Inertia*: An object will maintain a constant angular velocity unless acted on by an external torque *(moment)*.

2) **Law of Acceleration**: The angular acceleration of an object is produced by a torque *(moment)* directly proportional to that torque and inversely proportional to the object's moment of inertia.

3) **Law of Reaction**: For every torque *(moment)*, there is a reaction torque *(moment)* equal in magnitude and opposite in direction.

Calculating Force and Mechanical Advantage of Levers

Muscle force x Muscle force moment arm = Resistance force x Resistance force moment arm

Example: Calculate the muscle force required to lift a 30 lb. dumbbell given the following:

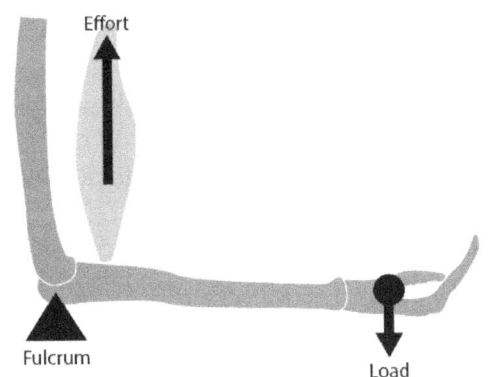

Muscle force (MF) = ?
Muscle force arm (MA) = 1" inch
Resistive force (RF) = 30 lbs.
Resistive force arm (RA) = 10" inches

MF x MA = RF x RA
MF x 1 = 30 x 10
MF = 30 x 10 ÷ 1
MF = 300 lbs.

If the resistive force arm were shortened to 5" then the muscle force needed to lift the weight would be 150 lbs.

If the muscle force arm was lengthened to 2" while keeping the resistive force arm at 10" then the muscle force needed to lift the weight would also be 150 lbs.

In a biceps curl (elbow flexion) the insertion point of the biceps tendon on the forearm dictates the length of the muscle force arm. If the tendon attaches further down the forearm, there is more of a mechanical advantage as demonstrated above.

Calculating Work and Power Output

Work = Newtons x Distance x Repetitions

Example: Calculate the work required to lift a 200 lb barbell a distance of 2 meters for 5 repetitions.

200 ÷ 2.2 = 90.9 Kg
90.9 x 9.8 = 891 Newtowns (N)
891 x 2 x 5 = 8,910 Joules (J) of work performed

Power Output = Work ÷ Time

Using the information above calculate the power output if an athlete performed the 5 repetitions at the given load in 10 seconds.

8,910 ÷ 20 = 445.5 Watts of power output

Training Principles

FITT-VP Principles: *Frequency, Intensity, Time, Type, Volume, Progression*

The FITT-VP principles of exercise prescription should be used to design Cardiorespiratory, Muscular, and Flexibility exercise programs. Variables should be adjusted as necessary to maintain progress and avoid stagnation in training.

Specificity of training: States the body will adapt to the demands that are placed upon it. *Only the muscles that are trained will adapt and change in response.* Resistance programs must target all muscles for which a training effect is desired.

SAID principle: Specific Adaptations to Imposed Demands
The type of demand placed on the body dictates the type of adaptation that will occur.

Progressive overload: The systematic increase in training frequency, volume, and intensity in various combinations. As the body adapts to a given stimulus, an increase in stimulus is required for further adaptations and improvements.

Variation in training: No one program should be used without changing the exercise stimulus over time. An example of increasing variety is periodized training.

Periodization: Division of a training program into smaller, progressive stages. Manipulation of the training variables *(volume, intensity, frequency, and rest intervals)* optimizes physiological outcomes while reducing the incidence of overtraining. Periodization allows for optimal training and recovery time. Timeframes for periodization programs are listed below.

- **Macrocycle**: *Annual plan*
- **Mesocycle**: *Monthly plan*
- **Microcycle**: *Weekly plan*

Prioritization of training: Training goals should be prioritized for each training cycle. It is difficult and not advised to train for all aspects of muscular fitness at once *(muscular endurance, strength, hypertrophy, power)*.

Overtraining syndrome (OTS): Excessive frequency, volume, or intensity of training, resulting in fatigue; also caused by a lack of proper rest and recovery. ***Also called over-reaching.***

Homeostasis: The ability or tendency of an organism or a cell to maintain internal equilibrium by adjusting its physiological processes. *When the body maintains a constant, steady state despite external changes such as exercise (physiological balance).*

Detraining or reversibility of conditioning refers to when a training stimulus is stopped the body gradually returns to its pre-conditioned state. It is a partial or complete reversal of the physiological adaptations gained through exercise. The phrase *"Use it or Lose it"* is a simple way to remember this concept.

Transfer specificity: States that every training activity has a percentage of carryover to other activities, but no conditioning activity has perfect carryover. Training is only 100% transferred when performing the exact targeted task *(running, swimming, surfing, throwing a ball, etc.)*
The optimal training program should maximize carryover to the sport or activity.

Mechanical specificity: The weights and movements placed on the body. The specific muscular requirements using different weights and movements that are performed to increase strength or endurance in certain body parts.

Neuromuscular specificity: The specific muscular contractions using different speeds and patterns that are performed to increase neuromuscular efficiency.

Metabolic specificity: Energy demand placed on the body.

General Adaptation Syndrome (GAS): (1) How the kinetic chain responds and adapts to imposed demands. (2) How the body responds and adapts to stress. GAS is broken down into the following (3) phases:

1) **Alarm phase**: The initial response to the imposed demands of exercise which last approximately 2-3 weeks. Neuromuscular adaptation is primarily taking place in this phase which can cause fatigue, weakness, and soreness as the body adapts. Initial increases in strength are from the neuromuscular adaptation, not actual structural, muscular changes.

2) **Adaptation phase**: The body adapts to the imposed stress of exercise by changing structures in the body (lasting approximately 4-12 weeks). During this phase muscle fibers increase in thickness and *intermuscular coordination* is improved which increases strength and the body's ability to perform the exercise movements.

3) **Exhaustion phase**: The body can no longer adapt to the imposed demands of the applied training stimulus. Further adaptations may halt, and the potential for physiological and structural breakdown increases. The risk of *overtraining syndrome (OTS)* also increases.

Rhabdomyolysis: Often a sign of overtraining this condition happens when a rapid breakdown of muscle tissue results in the release of intramuscular proteins *(myoglobin, myosin protein)* into the bloodstream. This can be potentially harmful to the kidneys and could lead to kidney failure and sometimes death in extreme cases. Symptoms of rhabdomyolysis include severe muscle aches, weakness, and extremely dark reddish-brown urine. If rhabdomyolysis is suspected, seek medical help immediately.

Valsalva maneuver: Moderate forceful exhalation against a closed glottis *(close mouth, pinch nose shut)* while pressing out as if blowing up a balloon. The Valsalva maneuver is commonly used in powerlifting to stabilize the trunk during exercises like the squat and deadlift. The Valsalva maneuver should be avoided by the general population as it increases intra-abdominal pressure, blood pressure and heart rate. This can be dangerous by hindering a person's cardiac output and cause dizziness or fainting.

Acute Variables

Acute variables are the components that specify how each exercise is to be performed. **The five acute program variables include**: *1) Choice of exercises, 2) Order of exercises, 3) Amount of resistance and number of repetitions, 4) Number of sets, and 5) Duration of rest periods between sets and exercises.* ***Changing the acute variables when necessary will help to ensure the body continues to experience the desired training adaptations.**

Choice of Exercises

Exercise selection: The process of choosing exercises that allow for achievement of the desired adaptation. **Exercises should be specific to the client's desired training goals.*

Primary exercises: Train the prime movers and are typically major muscle group exercises. **Deadlifts, squats, bench press, and pull-ups*

Assistance exercises: Train predominantly a single muscle group that aids in the movement produced by the prime movers. **Synergist and stabilizer muscles*

Multi-joint exercise: Involves two or more muscle groups and joints during the exercise. **Deadlifts, squats, power cleans, and bench press.*

Single-joint exercise: Isolate a particular muscle group involving one joint movement. **Bicep curls, knee extensions, and leg curls.*

Bilateral: Exercises or movements involving both limbs. **Barbell bench press*

Unilateral: Exercises or movements involving one limb. **One arm bicep curl.*
*Incorporating unilateral exercises will help maintain equal strength in both limbs and prevent bilateral differences that can occur with one limb working harder than the other.

Push exercises: Exercises involving the *"push"* muscle groups. **Bench press, squat, & abduction*

Pull exercises: Exercises involving the *"pull"* muscle groups. **Pull-ups, deadlifts, & adduction*

Order of Exercises

The **order of exercises** should be prioritized according to the **client's needs and goals**. Greater strength gains are seen in the exercises that are performed first due to the greater number of reps and sets *(volume)* one can perform when they are fresh. Ideally, an exercise session should start with the largest muscle group or most complex exercise and progress to smaller muscle groups and less complex movements. General recommendations for the order of exercises:

- Large muscle groups before small muscle groups
- Multi-joint before single-joint exercises
- Alternate push/pull exercises for total body sessions
- Alternate upper/lower body exercises for total body sessions
- Explosive/power type lifts & plyometric exercises before basic strength and single-joint
- Exercises for priority weak areas before exercises for strong areas
- Most intense to least intense

Resistance Training Modalities

Variable-Resistance equipment operates through a lever arm, cam, or pulley arrangement to alter the resistance throughout the exercise's range of motion (ROM). The purpose is to match the increases and decreases in strength *(strength curve)* through the entire range of motion (ROM) to ensure the muscle(s) are maximally contracted.

There are (3) Major Types of Strength Curves

- **Ascending**: More weight can be lifted if only the **Top half** of a repetition is performed. *Squats are an example of this strength curve.*

- **Descending**: More weight can be lifted if only the **Bottom half** of a repetition is performed. *Upright rowing is an example of this strength curve.*

- **Bell-shaped**: More weight can be lifted if only the **Middle portion** of a repetition is performed. *A bicep curl (elbow flexion) is an example of this strength curve.*

Dynamic Constant External Resistance training: The external resistance does not change, and both a lifting *(concentric)* phase, and a lowering *(eccentric)* phase occur during each repetition.

Dumbbells, Barbells, Kettlebells, Weight machines, Medicine balls, and other Free weights.

Static Resistance Devices: Refers to an *isometric* muscular action in which no change in the length of the muscle takes place *(joints do not move)*. This type of resistance training is normally performed against an immovable object such as a wall, barbell, or weight machine loaded beyond the maximal concentric strength of an individual.

*****Isometric exercises strengthen muscles fibers within 15° of the position being held.***

Isokinetic Devices allow one to maintain a maximum resistance throughout the whole ROM by controlling the speed of the movement. *These devices use friction, compressed air, pneumatics, or hydraulics.*

Needs Analysis for a Resistance Training Program

1) What is the main goal of the resistance training program?
2) What muscle groups need to be trained?
3) What are the basic energy sources *(anaerobic / aerobic)* that need to be trained?
4) What type of muscle action *(isometric / concentric / eccentric)* should be used?
5) What are the primary sites of injury for the particular sport or prior injury history of the individual?

Resistance Training Goals: *General health, muscular strength, muscular endurance, muscular hypertrophy, and/or muscular power.* ***Each of these desired outcomes requires a different program design to optimize the stated goals. Realistic expectations and time commitments should also be discussed with the client.***

Training Recommendations Based on Goals

A person's current fitness status provides a good indicator of the appropriate volume. Deconditioned or novice clients should begin with manageable volumes before progressing to advanced training volumes.

\	Muscular Strength	
Acute Variables	*Novice & Intermediate Individuals*	*Advanced Individuals*
Volume	1 - 3 sets per exercise	Multiple set programs with systematic variations in volume and intensity.
Intensity	60% - 70% of 1RM	Cycling load of 80% - 100% of 1RM
Repetitions	8 - 12 reps per set	Progressing to heavy loads of 1 - 6 reps
Rest period	2 - 3 min between sets for core lifts 1 - 2 min between sets for assistance exercises	2 - 3 min between sets for core lifts 1 - 2 min between sets for assistance lifts *Extended periods of rest may be necessary*
Frequency	Novice: 2 - 3 days per week Intermediate: 3 - 4 days per week	4 - 6 days per week

\	Muscular Hypertrophy	
Acute Variables	*Novice & Intermediate Individuals*	*Advanced Individuals*
Volume	1 - 3 sets per exercise	3 - 6 sets per exercise in a periodized manner
Intensity	70% - 85% of 1RM	70% - 100% of 1RM
Repetitions	8 - 12 reps	1 - 12 reps per set 6 - 12 reps for the majority
Rest period	1 - 2 minutes between sets	2 - 3 min between sets for heavy loading 1 - 2 min for moderate to moderate-high intensity
Frequency	Novice: 2 - 3 days per week Intermediate: Up to 4 days per week for split-routines	4 - 6 days per week

Acute Variables	Muscular Power	
	Novice & Intermediate Individuals	**Advanced Individuals**
Volume	1 - 3 sets per exercise	3 - 6 sets per exercise
Intensity	**Light to moderate loads** 30% - 60% of 1RM for upper body 0% - 60% of 1RM for lower body	**Heavy loading** *Necessary for increasing force 85% - 100% of 1RM **Light to moderate loads** 30% - 60% of 1RM for upper body 0% - 60% of 1RM for lower body
Repetitions	3 - 6 reps not to failure	1 - 6 reps in a periodized manner *Performed at an explosive velocity
Rest period	2 - 3 min between sets for primary exercises when intensity is high 1 - 2 min for assistance exercises or lower intensity	2 - 3 min between sets for primary exercises when intensity is high 1 - 2 min for assistance exercises or lower intensity
Frequency	Novice: 2 - 3 days per week Intermediate: 3 - 4 days per week	4 - 5 days per week

Training volume: The total amount of work performed within a specified time.
Volume = Reps x Sets x Resistance

Tempo: The amount of time that a muscle is actively producing tension during exercise movements.

Repetition Tempo refers to the speed with which each repetition is performed. Tempos are listed in seconds as *(eccentric portion / isometric (pause) / concentric portion)*.

Exercises don't have to follow the sequence listed. (Squats start with eccentric / Deadlifts start with concentric) but they are always recorded the same way starting with the eccentric portion.

Load: The amount of weight lifted or resistance used during training.
*As the *load* increases the *volume* decreases and *rest period* increases.
*As the *load* decreases the *volume* increases and *rest period* decreases.

Training intensity: An individual's level of effort compared with his or her maximal effort; usually expressed as a percentage.

Rest period: The time taken between sets or exercises to rest or recover.

Periodization of Exercise

Periodization refers to a systematic variation in acute program variables such as the prescribed volume and intensity during different phases of a resistance training program.

Linear Periodization: Classic or traditional strength and power programming that begins with high-volume, low-intensity training and progresses toward low-volume, high-intensity training. A traditional linear periodization program contains the following (4) phases:

1) *Hypertrophy phase*: High volume and short rest periods.
2) *Strength/Power phase*: Reduced volume but increased load and rest periods.
3) *Peaking phase*: Low volume but high load and longer rest periods.
4) *Recovery phase*: Low volume and load.

*See Table 14.5 on Page 398 of ACSM's Resources for the Personal Trainer - Fifth Edition for an example of a classic linear periodized program.

*Linear periodization is great to use for untrained clients as it progresses them systematically thru each phase ensuring proper adaptations are met before moving to the next phase. This helps to prevent the risk of injury and overtraining.

Reverse Linear Periodization programs follow the traditional linear tenants in reverse order. This type of periodization is beneficial when muscular endurance is the primary goal.

Nonlinear Periodization / Daily Undulating Periodization (DUP): A form of periodization that provides changes in the acute variables *(volume / intensity)* of workouts to achieve different goals on a daily or weekly basis. **e.g. Power on Monday, Endurance on Wednesday, and Strength on Friday.* A typical nonlinear program would follow a 12 week mesocycle. Nonlinear (DUP) programs go by a set number of workouts completed *(e.g. 48)* rather than counting the number of weeks.

*See Table 14.6 on Page 400 of ACSM's Resources for the Personal Trainer - Fifth Edition for an example of a Nonlinear periodized program.

Unplanned/Flexible Nonlinear Periodization: Allows variation to the program so that each workout is performed based on the client's readiness to train *(fatigue level, psychological state, fitness)*. A *light, moderate, power, or heavy* training protocol will be selected based on the state of the client at the time of the session. This type of periodization aims to optimize each training session. **If the client is well rested and has a lot of energy then a power or heavy lifting day can be performed, whereas a fatigued client should perform a lighter workout.*

Progression and Regression of Exercises

Exercise technique is the most important aspect of resistance training for beginners. Correct technique should be significantly emphasized, and the resistance and volume should be kept low for beginners. As clients become accustomed to a given stimulus or dose of exercise, additional exercise stress should be added gradually by adjusting the acute variables. Multiple sets are recommended once the client has built-up their initial base and technique. As the client's skill and experience level improve, more technical exercises can be added to their program.

See Figures 14.5A - 14.5O from Pages 404 - 410 of ACSM's Resources for the Personal Trainer - Fifth Edition for examples of 15 basic exercises: (A) Squat, (B) Supine leg press, (C) 45° Leg press, (D) Lunge, (E) Leg extensions, (F) Leg curls, (G) Machine vertical bench press, (H) Smith supine bench press, (I) Free-weight supine bench press, (J) Dumbbell bench press, (K) Machine seated rows, (L) Front lat pull-down, (M) Dumbbell are curls, (N) Barbell arm curls, and (O) Triceps push-down.

Progression of exercises: Describes the progressive stages of making an exercise more difficult or challenging. Usually by creating additional instability which enhances proprioception & neuromuscular control.

Example Progressions

- Easy to Hard
- Slow to Fast
- Static to Dynamic
- Stable to Unstable
- Simple to Complex
- Eyes Open to Eyes Closed
- Two Arms/Legs to Single-Arm/Leg
- Known to Unknown (cognitive task)
- Body Weight to Loaded Movements

Progressing an individual too quickly can lead to improper movement patterns and increase the risk of injury. A client must be able to perform an exercise with proper form and technique before progressing to a more challenging version or exercise.

Regression of exercises: Describes regressing an exercise making it easier to perform. Usually by creating a more stable base of support *(i.e., both feet on the ground)*.

If a client is unable to perform a standard push-up you could regress the movement to have them perform it with their knees on the ground instead. Once enough strength has been built up they could progress to a traditional push-up and even further to performing push-ups with feet on a bench or stability ball.

Spotting Techniques

Proper spotting techniques reassure the client while performing an exercise and reduce the risk of injury during that exercise. A verbal explanation along with a demonstration of proper lifting technique by the fitness professional prior to the client performing the actual exercise is beneficial. It will help the client to understand and maintain proper position, form, technique, and control during the movement. Using the **right/wrong method** can also be helpful where the trainer shows a client an incorrect position and then what the correct position looks like. Personal trainers should be familiar with a large number of exercises and know how to properly teach, spot, and cue each exercise so that clients understand and follow through with correct performance.

Below is a checklist for proper spotting technique:

- Know proper exercise and spotting techniques.
- Know how many repetitions the lifter intends to do before performing the set.
- Make sure to have a good base of support and are strong enough to assist the lifter with the resistance being used.
- Be attentive to the lifter at all times.
- Stop lifters if they break form or have improper technique.
- Provide just enough assistance for the client to successfully complete the lift, helping them through any *"sticking point."*
- Keep hands on or close to the weight being lifted. *When using a barbell a closed alternated grip is recommended to prevent the bar from rolling out of hands.*
- Both the spotter(s) and the client / lifter must communicate effectively before and during the lift to ensure safety and expectations during the lift.
- **Spot at the client's forearms near the wrists when using dumbbells, especially for chest press and overhead press exercises.** Certain exercises require spotting with hands on the dumbbell itself such as a dumbbell pullover or overhead triceps extension.
- Know the plan of action if a serious injury occurs.

Spotting procedures often require physical interaction between the trainer and client. ***Always ask your clients before physically touching them to ensure they are comfortable with it.***

Cueing

Cueing is both verbal and nonverbal communication that is used to evoke an action response from participants. Always phrase cues positively and avoid negative connotations such as *"don't"* Common observations and appropriate cues are listed below:

Observation: A client's knees cave in *(adduct)* during a squat exercise.
Cue: "Keep your knees in line with your second toe throughout the movement."

Observation: A client's lower back begins to arch while performing push-ups.
Cue: "Tuck your hips and brace your core." *(abdominal bracing)*

Observation: A client holds their breath while performing static stretches.
Cue: "Continue to breathe slowly to help relax the muscles being stretched."

General Cardiorespiratory Training Principles

Cardiorespiratory *(aerobic)* endurance refers to the ability of the heart, blood vessels *(circulatory system)*, and lungs *(respiratory system)* to provide oxygen to the body during sustained physical activity.

Maximal oxygen consumption *(VO$_2$Max)* is a good indicator of an individual's aerobic fitness, the higher the VO$_2$Max, the greater the individual's aerobic capacity.

Overload of the cardiovascular and respiratory systems is required to have beneficial adaptations in cardiorespiratory endurance. Enhancing the body's ability to deliver and utilize oxygen for metabolic processes allows one to do more work.

Regression *(De-adaptation)* refers to the loss of physiological adaptation by reducing the overload on the system *(body begins to regress to pretraining status)*. This can occur if a client is injured or has to decrease their exercise below the *"threshold level."*

Retrogression refers to the decrease in physiological capacities resulting from excessive stress that is placed on the cardiorespiratory system. **The Personal Trainer must balance the FITT-VP principles of the workouts to avoid over-challenging the client beyond an appropriate amount of overload.*

Intensity: Varies depending on individual fitness level. Sedentary individuals who are very deconditioned should start with low intensity *(30% - 39% of HRR or VO$_2$R)*. Habitually active individuals can train at higher intensities *(60% - 89% of HRR or VO$_2$R)*.

Progression: Depends on the individual's health status, training response, current fitness level, and the exercise program goals.

Implementation of effective cardiorespiratory endurance training programs requires the Personal Trainer to have knowledge of the current scientific basis of exercise.

*The Personal Trainer should always instruct clients about proper posture and body alignment during cardiorespiratory training. Proper biomechanics will ensure optimal efficiency and reduce the risk of injury.

Benefits of Cardiorespiratory Fitness

- Improved work, recreational, and sports performance
- Decreased fatigue in daily activities
- Enhanced sense of well-being
- Improved body composition

Improved cardiorespiratory function:

- Increased maximal oxygen uptake
- Increased maximal cardiac output (Q) & stroke volume (SV)
- Increased capillary density in skeletal muscle
- Increased mitochondrial density
- Increased lactate threshold
- Lower heart rate (HR) and blood pressure (BP) at a fixed submaximal work rate
- Lower myocardial oxygen demand at a fixed submaximal work rate

Improved immune function:

- Improved glucose tolerance and insulin sensitivity

Improved blood lipid profile:

- Decreased triglycerides
- Decreased postprandial lipemia
- Increased high-density lipoprotein (HDL) cholesterol

Decreased risk of the following:

- Mortality from all causes
- Coronary artery disease
- Cancer (colon, perhaps breast and prostate)
- Hypertension
- Noninsulin-dependent diabetes mellitus
- Osteoporosis
- Anxiety
- Depression

FITT-VP Recommendations for Cardiorespiratory Exercise	
Frequency	≥ 5 days per week of moderate exercise, or ≥ 3 days per week of vigorous exercise, or a combination of moderate and vigorous exercise on ≥ 3 - 5 days per week.
Intensity	Moderate and/or vigorous-intensity exercise for most adults
Time	30 - 60 min per day *(150 min per week)* of purposeful moderate exercise, or 20 - 60 min per day *(75 min per week)* of vigorous exercise, or a combination of moderate and vigorous exercise per day for most adults. < 20 min per day *(< 150 min per week)* of exercise can be beneficial for previously sedentary persons.
Type	Regular, purposeful exercise that involves major muscle groups and is continuous and rhythmic in nature.
Volume	≥ 500 – 1,000 Metabolic equivalents (MET) per week
Pattern	One continuous session per day or multiple ≥ 10 min sessions to accumulate the desired duration and volume of exercise per day. < 10 min per session may yield favorable adaptation in very deconditioned individuals
Progression	Gradual progression of exercise volume by adjusting exercise duration, frequency, and/or intensity until desired exercise goal *(maintenance)* is attained.

*A cardiorespiratory session includes a warm-up, and endurance phase, and a cool-down.

*Examples of cardiorespiratory endurance programs are found in Tables 15.12 & 15.13 from Pages 442 - 445 of ACSM's Resources for the Personal Trainer - Fifth Edition.

*MET calculations for exercise volume can be found in Box 15.5 on Pages 440 & 441 of ACSM's Resources for the Personal Trainer - Fifth Edition.

Grouping of Cardiorespiratory Exercise and Activities

Exercise Group	Exercise Description	Recommended for	Examples
A	Endurance activities requiring minimal skill or physical fitness to perform	All Adults	Walking, leisurely cycling, aqua-aerobics, slow dancing
B	Vigorous-intensity endurance activities requiring minimal skill	Adults *(per the preparticipation screening guidelines)* who are habitually physically active and/or at least average physical fitness	Jogging, running, rowing, aerobics, spinning, elliptical exercise, stepping exercise, fast dancing
C	Endurance activities requiring skill to perform	Adults with acquired skill and/or at least average physical fitness levels	Swimming, cross-country skiing, skating
D	Recreational sports	Adults with a regular exercise program and at least average physical fitness	Racquet sports, basketball, soccer, downhill skiing, hiking

Physiological Adaptations to Aerobic Conditioning in Untrained Individuals

Variable	Submaximal Effort	Maximal Effort
VO_2Max	No change	Increases
Resting Heart Rate (RHR)	Decreases	Increases
Exercise Heart Rate (EHR)	Decreases	Increases
Maximum Heart Rate (MHR)	No change	No change
a-vO_2 difference	Increases	Increases
Maximum Minute Ventilation	Decreases	Increases
Stroke Volume (SV)	Decreases	Increases
Cardiac Output (Q)	Decreases	Increases
Blood Volume	Increases	Increases
Systolic Blood Pressure (SBP)	Decreases	No change or Increases
Blood Lactate	Decreases	Increases
Oxidative capacity of skeletal muscle	Decreases	Increases

Flexibility

Flexibility refers to the normal extensibility of soft tissue and the degree to which a joint moves throughout a normal, pain-free range of motion (ROM). *When flexibility is limited, faulty movement patterns can arise and are reinforced during exercise.*

Static flexibility is the range of possible movement a joint and surrounding muscles have during a passive movement.

Dynamic flexibility refers to the available range of motion (ROM) during active movements and requires voluntary muscular actions.

Relative flexibility: The human movement system's way of finding the path of least resistance during movement.

Mobility is the freedom of an individual's limb to move through the desired range of motion (ROM).

Hypermobility refers to a joint that moves beyond its normal range of motion due to laxity of the ligaments and joint.

Factors that determine flexibility include: Joint structure, health of soft tissue around the joint, length of antagonist muscles, temperature of the tissues being stretched, and viscoelastic *(rubber-band like)* properties of the tissues surrounding the joint.

Goniometry is used to measure the total amount of available range of motion at a specific joint.

Evaluating a client's flexibility using a goniometry assessment is an essential part of developing their exercise program. The following important information is gathered to assist with program development.

- Initial range of motion (ROM) prior to the start of the exercise program.
- Baseline measurements from which plans can be made for future exercise goals.
- Immediate range of motion (ROM) feedback.
- Identification of muscular imbalances.

Flexibility training aims to increase the range of motion (ROM) around a joint.
Normal range of motion (ROM) does not guarantee normal movement. Dynamic flexibility involves mobility *(movement)* through a range of motion (ROM) which enhances motor control, balance, and coordination. These aspects transfer well to help maximize performance.

Examples of types of stretching are shown in Figures 16.2 through 16.40 from Pages 454 - 468 of ACSM's Resources for the Personal Trainer - Fifth Edition.

Stretching Techniques

Active stretch: The person stretching supplies the force of the stretch.

Passive stretching: The person stretching is not actively involved. The individual assumes a position and then either holds it with another part of the body or with assistance from a partner or some other apparatus *(resistance band, towel)*. **The goal is to move the individual slowly into the stretch to prevent a forceful action and possible injury.*

Static stretching: Slowly move into position then holding that stretch at the point of tightness *(mild discomfort)* for **10 – 30 seconds *(30-60 seconds for older adults)***. Static stretches should focus on the overactive *(tight, shortened)* muscles that are identified through assessments. Clients should be reminded to avoid holding breath and continue to breathe during stretches. **Static stretching may temporarily reduce power and strength. It is recommended that static stretching be performed after any exercise or sport where strength and power are important.*

Dynamic stretching: Moving parts of the body in a controlled manner through a full range of motion (ROM) while gradually increasing the reach and/or speed of movement. Dynamic stretching performed during the warm-up should use movement patterns similar to the conditioning phase the individual is preparing for. **Perform 5 – 12 repetitions of each movement while progressively increasing the ROM on each repetition.*

Proprioceptive Neuromuscular Facilitation (PNF): Involves both stretching and contracting the targeted muscle group. The most common PNF technique is ***contract-relax.*** Following the preliminary passive stretch, the muscle is isometrically contracted at 20% - 75% intensity for 6 seconds, relaxed for 2 - 3 seconds, and then passively moved into the final stretch that is held for 10 - 30 seconds. **PNF is most effective with the use of a trainer to assist the client through the stretch.*

Ballistic stretching: Involves a bouncing or jerky type movement to reach the muscle's ROM limits. This type of stretching is not appropriate for the general population but may be suitable for athletes where explosive movements are critical to their sport. **The risk of injury is higher with ballistic stretching if not performed properly.*

Flexibility exercises have the potential to improve joint range of motion (ROM) and physical function.

Stretching Tips

- Hold stretches for appropriate timeframes *(min 30 seconds)* to allow for the inhibitory response and muscle relaxation caused by Golgi Tendon Organs (GTO's).
- Always breathe during stretches and avoid tensing up and holding breath.
- Joints should never be taken past their normal range of motion while performing these various stretching techniques.

Designing a Flexibility Program

There are three preliminary training guidelines involved with designing a flexibility program. The guidelines include a *warm-up, breathing, and posture.*

Warm-up: An active warm-up reduces the resistance of stretching. Using a treadmill for walking / running, an elliptical machine, stationary cycling, and rowing are good options to warm-up the muscles. This prepares the body for any stretching and/or conditioning that follows. Stretching at the end of a workout when the muscles are warm is recommended. **Warm muscle tissue increases the elastic properties and ability to stretch.*

Breathing: Purposeful and controlled breathing during stretching allows the body to relax *(reduce stress levels)* and decreases muscle tension. This allows for a deeper stretch and greater reduction of stiffness in the body. **Remind clients to exhale slowly as they move into a stretch, continue slow controlled breathing during the stretch, and then inhale as they come out of the stretch.*

Posture: Maintaining proper body alignment when performing stretching techniques ensures effectiveness of the stretch and reduces the chance of injury. Correct postural alignment includes *maintaining a neutral position of the spine, keeping shoulders back and away from the ears, and hips in a neutral and level position.*

FITT-VP Principles for Flexibility

- **Frequency**: Stretching activities should be included a minimum of 2 - 3 days per week for most adults. **A daily flexibility and mobility routine are most effective.*
- **Intensity**: A stretch should never be painful. Stretches should be held to a point of mild muscle tightness without excessive discomfort *(13 – 15 on RPE scale / somewhat hard to hard).* If there is pain or excessive discomfort, the stretch should be released back to a point of mild tightness.
- **Time**: At least 10 minutes is recommended per session. **All the major muscle-tendon groups should be targeted with 2 - 4 repetitions for each stretch.*
- **Type**: Static stretching *(active and passive),* dynamic or slow movement stretching, and proprioceptive neuromuscular facilitation (PNF).
- **Volume**: Each flexibility exercise should be held at the point of tightness for 10 - 30 seconds per joint. **The aim is to accumulate a total of 60 seconds of stretching per joint.**
- **Progression**: Recommendations for optimal progression are unknown and will vary depending on each individual.

*Sample stretching programs are shown in Boxes 16.1 – 16.3 on Pages 471 – 473 of ACSM's Resources for the Personal Trainer - Fifth Edition

Self-Myofascial Release (SMR) is a manual massage technique used to eliminate general fascial restrictions. SMR can help alleviate the discomfort associated trigger points *(tender spots)* within the myofascial and relax hypertonic areas within the soft tissue. SMR is typically performed with a device such as a foam roller. *Lacrosse balls, softballs, and tennis balls are also commonly used.*

Fascia: A strong web of connective tissue that wraps and surrounds muscle fibers, bones, nerves, and blood vessels. The myofascial system covers individual muscles as well as connecting groups of larger muscles together. It provides structural support and protection. *Plural form is **Fasciae**.*

Recent studies have shown that SMR can help improve range of motion (ROM) without causing performance decrements (as seen with static stretching) when done prior to activity.

Common SMR form mistakes include the following:

- Rolling too quickly.
- Not identifying the trigger point / tender spot.
- Not holding static pressure on the trigger point / tender spot.
  Holding with no movement on trigger point helps to release it.
- Tensing the body in the presence of discomfort.
  Relax the muscle and focus on deep controlled breathing.

Alignment Issues and Soft Tissue Targets	
Alignment Fault	*Self-Myofascial Release and Stretching Targets*
Excessive kyphosis of the thoracic spine	Pectoralis major and minor / latissimus dorsi /abdominals
Internal rotation of the shoulders	Pectoralis major and minor / latissimus dorsi
Posterior pelvic tilt	Hamstrings /abdominals
Hyperextension of the lumbar spine (Lordosis)	Quadratus lumborum / quadriceps / iliopsoas

Stability and Mobility

Stability: Characteristic of the body's joints or posture that represents resistance to change of position.

Mobility: The degree to which an articulation is allowed to move before being restricted by surrounding tissues. ***Proximal** stability promotes **Distal** mobility*

<u>Mobilizer Muscles Characteristics</u>
- Fast twitch
- Fatigues easily
- Superficial
- Relatively small proprioceptive role
- High force production
- Prone to hold excess tension / shorten
- Concentric
- Gross movement (large movements)

<u>Stabilizer Muscles Characteristics</u>
- Slow twitch
- Resistant to fatigue
- Deep
- Major contributor to proprioception
- Low force production
- Prone to inhibition / weakness
- Isometric / Eccentric
- Joint stabilization

Stability and Mobility points of the kinetic chain are described below:
- Glenohumeral: Mobility
- Scapulothoracic: Stability
- Thoracic Spine: Mobility
- Lumbar Spine: Stability
- Hip: Mobility
- Knee: Stability
- Ankle: Mobility
- Foot: Stability

Optimal stabilization strategies require the following:
1) A stable base from which forces are transferred.
2) Adequate muscular capacity *(strength and endurance)*.
3) Central nervous system (CNS) programming *(integration of sensory input)* that produces synchronous activation of the muscles.

Proprioception is the sense of knowing where one's body is in space and is composed of static *(joint position sense)* and dynamic *(kinesthetic movement sense)*.

Motor control is developed through enhancing proprioceptive acuity and grooving proper movement patterns through practice.

Sensorimotor system consists of the sensory system and the motor control system. These systems work together to control movement, balance, posture, and joint stability.

Abdominal Bracing and Breathing Techniques

Abdominal bracing involves an isometric contraction of the core muscles to stabilize the spine. Clients should be instructed to pre-contract *"brace"* their core prior to performing isometric exercises such as a plank or isotonic movements such as squatting. The common cue *"pretend you are about to be hit in the stomach."* can help clients activate the correct muscles.

*The intensity of the brace should be adjusted to the relative intensity of the exercise.
The goal is to protect the spine without affecting proper mobility. A body weight squat requires minimal bracing where a 1RM squat requires near maximal bracing to maintain spinal integrity.

Diaphragmatic breathing involves contracting the diaphragm muscles to expand the rib cage and abdomen. This type of controlled *deep breathing* optimizes respiratory muscle function *(improved capacity and time to fatigue)* and core stability *(the diaphragm is the "roof" of the core muscles)*.

*Abdominal bracing should occur in concert with diaphragmatic breathing during isometric exercise and dynamic movements with low load. This can help improve the coordination of the diaphragm during tasks of core stabilization.

For most exercises, the client should **inhale during the eccentric phase** *(less stressful phase)* of the lift and **exhale during the concentric phase** or any *"sticking point"* of the lift.

Assessments and Corrections

The **Hi-Lo breathing assessment** can be performed to check and correct any breathing pattern problems a client has. The client places one hand on their sternum *(chest)* and one hand on their upper abdomen. The client is then instructed to perform 10 breathing cycles. **The hand on the upper abdomen should rise before the hand on the chest.** The hand on the chest should only move slightly forward and not upward toward the chin.

The **wall plank-and-roll (WPR)** is an assessment of lumbar *(core)* stability and rotational control. Once the client demonstrates sufficient stability for the wall roll, they can progress to performing a side plank from the knees and ultimately to a full body side plank. **Isometric endurance exercises should be repeated for sets of short-duration holds** *(8 – 10 seconds)* **rather than one prolonged hold** *(> 30 seconds)* **to optimize their effectiveness.**

*Assessment of rolling patterns along with corrective techniques and verbal cues are in Tables 17.9 – 17.11 on Page 494 of ACSM's Resources for the Personal Trainer - Fifth Edition.

Clients should be encouraged to be mindful *(aware)* of any lifestyle factors contributing to compensations or muscle imbalances they may have. Our bodies take the shape of the positions we are in most often. Improving the ergonomics of their work environment, setting a daily alarm as a reminder to stand and walk around, practicing diaphragmatic breathing, and foam rolling while watching TV at night can go a long way in getting back into proper alignment.

Alignment Fault Checklist and Associated Weak or Inhibited Stabilizing Muscles

- **Loss of cervical neutral**: Head positioned in front of the body or tilting up or down.
  Weak muscles include deep cervical flexors (longus colli, capitis).

- **Loss of thoracic extension**: Rounding of the thoracic spine.
  Weak muscles include the middle and lower trapezius.

- **Internal rotation of the shoulders**:
  Weak muscles include the external rotators of the shoulder (infraspinatus).

- **Posterior pelvic tilt**: Loss of neutral lordosis or flattening of the lumbar spine.
  Weak muscles include gluteus medius and maximus; multifidus.

- **Anterior pelvic tilt**: Excessive arching of the low back.
  Weak muscles include gluteus medius and maximus; transverse abdominis.

- **Knee valgus**: Knees collapsing inward.
  Weak muscles include gluteus medius and maximus.

Corrective exercises for alignment and core stabilization issues are shown in Figures 17.3 – 17.11 on Pages 495 – 499 of ACSM's Resources for the Personal Trainer - Fifth Edition.

Instability (Balance) Training

Instability training challenges a client's ability to maintain balance while challenging the client's center of gravity (COG). The goal of balance training is to improve stability, sensory acuity, and proprioception. The difficulty of the exercise should be selected based on the client's relative functional capacity. Clients should be able to maintain optimal alignment without significant swaying for 30 seconds on each exercise before progressing to a more difficult task.

Instability Progressions

- Wide staggered stance to Narrow staggered stance
- Two-leg to Single-leg
- Eyes open to Eyes closed
- Stable to Unstable
- Static to Dynamic

Table 17.14 on Page 500 of ACSM's Resources for the Personal Trainer - Fifth Edition shows a systematic approach to instability training.

Advanced Resistance Training Techniques

Heavy and forced negatives target the eccentric phase of an exercise with a slow cadence of 3 – 4 seconds. Muscles maintain greater strength during the eccentric phase even when fatigued on the concentric portion. The goal is to load the eccentric phase more than the concentric. This can be accomplished by *forced negatives* where the trainer applies manual force to the eccentric *(negative)* portion of a lift, using bilateral lifts for the concentric and single limb for the eccentric, or helping the client during the concentric and letting them lower the weight on their own.

Functional isometrics can be used to target any *"sticking point"* or weak area in the range of motion (ROM) of a lift. The client pushes or pulls maximally for 2 – 6 seconds against an immovable object such as a barbell blocked by pins which are set at the targeted area of the range of motion (ROM). *This is commonly used for bench press, deadlifts, squats, and clean pulls.*

Partial repetitions are performed at a partial range of motion (ROM) either in the area of maximal strength or near the *"sticking point."* The goal is to increase strength at the specified ROM and ultimately the full range of motion (ROM). Partial reps can also be used once the full ROM can no longer be performed unassisted due to fatigue.

Variable resistance training (VRT) is performed by altering the loading throughout the ROM. *Specific machines with cams that vary, elastic bands, and chains are commonly used in VRT.*

Forced repetitions are completed with assistance from a spotter or via self-spotting beyond one's normal capacity. The goal is to extend the set beyond failure in hopes of providing greater increases in muscle strength, endurance, and hypertrophy. *They are commonly used at the end of a set once momentary muscular failure has occurred with traditional reps.*

Contrast loading involves including low, moderate, and high reps within a single training session. Heavy resistance is usually lifted first followed by light or moderate weight. The goal is to recruit as many muscle fibers as possible with heavy weights then stimulate circulatory/metabolic growth factors with low-to-moderate weight and high repetitions.

Breakdown sets involve a rapid reduction in weight with minimal rest thereby allowing the client to extend a set by performing additional repetitions beyond fatigue. *Breakdown sets are commonly used to enhance muscle hypertrophy and endurance.*

Combining exercises involve performing two or more exercises consecutively or simultaneously with minimal rest. *Olympic lifts, kettlebell clean & press, dumbbell squat to press, and burpees with push-ups are some examples.* **Supersets (2), Tri-sets (3), and giant sets (4 or more)** can also be used to perform consecutive exercises that target the same or opposing muscle groups.

Quality training involves reducing the rest interval lengths within specific loading/volume parameters as training progresses.

Discontinuous sets include rest intervals in between repetitions. The goal is to increase the quality and effort of each repetition by maximizing acute force and power output.

Motion-specific training (functional training) involves the use of exercises that train specific movements. The goal is to increase primarily core stabilizer muscle strength and not the prime movers *(although there could be a secondary strength-building effect)*. *Bands, medicine balls, dumbbells, kettlebells, stability balls, ropes, TRX (suspension), and other devices can be used to load the specific movements.*

Advanced resistance training recommendations for strength, hypertrophy, endurance, and power are in Table 19.1 on Pages 525 & 526 of ACSM's Resources for the Personal Trainer - Fifth Edition.

Health-related components of fitness include *muscle strength and endurance, aerobic endurance, flexibility, and body composition.*

Skill-related components of fitness include *power, speed, agility, balance, reaction time, and coordination.*

Basic knowledge of biomechanics is critical for the Personal Trainer to make exercises easier *(regression)* or more difficult *(progression)* in the absence of adding external resistance.

Resistance training is any method or form of exercise requiring the client to exert a force against resistance.

Strength Implements such as *kettlebells, sleds, kegs, log bars, farmer's walk bars, thick bars, super yoke, sledge hammers, tires, stones, sandbags, heavy bags, battling ropes, and chains* can be used in advanced strength and conditioning programs. *Many of these strength implements can help to increase grip strength and also provide unbalanced resistance which helps to activate the stabilizer muscles along with the prime movers.*

Olympic lifts are total-body resistance exercises the recruit most major muscle groups. Several variations of the snatch, clean, and jerk are used. *Olympic lifts are the most complex resistance exercise to perform and are also considered most effective for increasing total-body power.*

Due to the complexity of Olympic lifts, Personal Trainers should have advanced training and instruction before using with clients.

Technical aspects of performing various Olympic lifts are described in Boxes 19.2 & 19.3 on Pages 535 - 536 of ACSM's Resources for the Personal Trainer - Fifth Edition.

Plyometric Training

Plyometric training refers to exercises that link strength with speed of movement to produce power *(activities in which muscles exert maximum force in short intervals of time, with the goal of increasing power)*. Plyometric exercise is a quick, powerful movement using a pre-stretch, or countermovement, that involves the **Stretch-Shortening Cycle (SSC).**

The **Stretch-Shortening Cycle (SSC)** combines mechanical and neurophysiological mechanisms and is the basis of plyometric exercise. A rapid eccentric muscle action stimulates the stretch reflex and storage of elastic energy, which increases the force produced during the subsequent concentric action. *Like pulling a rubber band back and releasing the stored **"elastic energy."***

SSC involves the following (3) phases:

1) **Eccentric** muscle contraction *(loading of the muscle / stretch of the agonist)*
2) **Amortization** *(pause between phases (isometric) / transition phase)*
3) **Concentric** muscle contraction *(release of stored energy / shortening of the agonist)*

A high stretch rate of the musculotendinous results in greater muscle recruitment and activity during the stretch-shortening cycle concentric phase. *Greater force is generated in a running long jump as compared to a static jump due to the higher stretch rate (eccentric phase) generated from the approach and take-off.*

Plyometric exercises consist of *jumps-in-place, standing jumps, multiple hops/jumps, bounding, box drills, depth jumps, plyo push-ups, and throws.* ***The vertical jump test is one of the most common power assessments used for athletes.***

Plyometric training variables include *exercise selection, order, intensity, volume, frequency, and rest intervals.*

Factors to consider when designing a plyometric program:

- **Quality of training**: Each rep should be performed with maximal effort, minimal amortization, and maximal velocity.
- **Exercise selection**: The selection should be as specific to the demands of the sport/activity as possible comprising unilateral and bilateral drills.
- Plyometric training should take place in an area with sufficient space. *(horizontal length 30-40 yards / ceiling height higher than maximal reach)*
- Proper technique should always be instructed.
- Sufficient rest should be given when peak power is the goal.
- Gradual progression entails increases in intensity via the addition of complex exercises and some external loading. Low-intensity and moderate intensity drills should be mastered before progressing to high-intensity drills.
- Volume can be increased with the number of contacts per session and should be progressed gradually.
- High-intensity workouts require longer recovery period in between workouts.
- Ensure the client has proper jumping, landing, and throwing technique.

Plyometric training volume is usually measured in contacts per session *(how many times a foot or feet contact the surface)*. Appropriate plyometric training volumes are listed below:

- **Beginner** *(no experience)*: 80 to 100 contacts per session
- **Intermediate** *(some experience)*: 100 to 120 contacts per session
- **Advanced** *(considerable experience)*: 120 to 140 contacts per session

1:5 work-to-rest ratios are appropriate for **low- to moderate-intensity plyometric exercises.*
1:10 work-to-rest ratios are recommended for **high-intensity plyometric exercises.*
*48 to 72 hours between plyometric sessions is a typical recovery timeline.
(Typically 1 – 4 sessions per week)

When performing **lower body plyometrics,** the **shoulders should be over the knees and knees over the toes** during the landing. Inward movement of the knees *(dynamic valgus)* when landing significantly increases the likelihood of injury.

Depth jumps are generally considered the most intense. The recommended height for depth jumps ranges from 8 – 45 inches *(20 – 115 cm)*. Starting with **8 – 16 inches *(20 – 40 cm)*** with gradual progression.

Ballistic resistance training is a plyometric modality aimed at increasing muscle power and strength. Ballistic training aims to *minimize deceleration* by having the client maximally accelerate the bar / body weight throughout the full ROM. This results in releasing the load at the end of the concentric contraction *(jumping off ground / throwing and object)*.

Common ballistic exercises include *jump squats, bench press throws, medicine ball throws, and shoulder press throws.* **Peak power is produced at loads corresponding to 15% - 60% of 1RM for the jump squat and bench press throw.*

Complex training is a combination of high-intensity resistance training followed by plyometrics *(postactivation potentiation)*. Traditional resistance training can be combined with plyometrics to enhance muscular power. When integrating resistance training and plyometrics, the intensity should be alternated accordingly on different training days. **High-intensity resistance training days should include low-intensity plyometrics and vice versa.*

Anaerobic conditioning refers to high-intensity muscle endurance capacity *(the ability to perform near-maximal to maximal exercise for an extended period of time)*. Exercises targeting speed, power, and strength endurance are used. **Drills consist of longer sprints, repeated sprints, interval sprints, and relays. *The 300-yard shuttle and the line drill can be used to assess anaerobic capacity.*

*1:1 work-to-rest ratios target aerobic capacity.
*1:5 or 1:10 work-to-rest ratios target anaerobic conditioning.

Circuit training involves performing several exercises in a short period of time yielding substantial metabolic and cardiovascular responses that could improve aerobic capacity.

Adaptations to Anaerobic Training Programs

Anaerobic training is characterized by intermittent bouts of high-intensity exercise. This type of training requires **adenosine triphosphate (ATP)** to be regenerated at a faster rate than the aerobic energy system is capable of. The **anaerobic energy systems** *(anaerobic alactic & anaerobic lactic systems)* do not require oxygen and are used for anaerobic training *(short durations of high-intensity exercise)*.

The following are beneficial adaptations resulting from anaerobic training modalities: *Improvements in muscular strength, power, hypertrophy, muscular endurance, body composition, flexibility, aerobic capacity, motor skills, and coordination.*

Neural adaptations *(improved motor learning & coordination)* are fundamental to optimizing athletic performance. Muscular speed and power depend greatly on optimal neural recruitment for maximal performance. Anaerobic training can elicit changes to the neuromuscular system to improve performance. Neural adaptions typically occur before any structural changes in skeletal muscle *(hypertrophy)*. **This explains the strength gains seen in the early part of an exercise program of an untrained individual (6-10 weeks).*

All-or-None Principle states that when a stimulus exceeds the *"threshold potential,"* the nerve or muscle fiber will give a complete response or no response *(there is no in between)*. This doesn't mean that it gives a full force contraction response for any resistance applied. The force of muscle contraction is varied depending on the number of motor units/muscle fibers that are activated. **Lifting a small amount of weight on a biceps curl requires fewer motor units than lifting a heavier weight with the same movement.*

As muscle size increases, it does not require as much neural activation to lift a given load. **Smaller muscles rely more on firing rates of motor units and larger muscles rely more on the recruitment of motor units to enhance force production.*

Henneman's size principle states that under load, **motor units are recruited from smallest to largest.** In practice, this means that slow-twitch, low-force, fatigue-resistant muscle fibers are activated before fast-twitch, high-force, less fatigue-resistant muscle fibers.

Selective recruitment inhibits the lower-threshold motor units and activates higher-threshold motor units in their place. This selective recruitment is used for explosive movements when force production is required at very high speeds for the expression of muscular power *(such as a vertical high jump)*.

With heavy resistance training, all muscle fibers get larger *(hypertrophy)* because motor units are recruited in a sequential order by their size to produce high levels of force. In advanced lifters, the central nervous system may adapt by allowing well-trained athletes to recruit some motor units in a nonconsecutive order, by recruiting larger ones first to promote greater production of power or speed in a movement.

Speed and Agility Training

Speed is the change in distance over time. **Maximal speed attainment takes 20 – 40 meters*, so **acceleration** *(ability to increase velocity)* is a critical training component. **The 40-yard dash is the most common speed assessment.*

Sprint speed can be increased by an *increase in stride length* or in *stride frequency (number of foot contacts per period of time)*. One must produce large amounts of force within a short amount of time. This results in longer stride lengths at a faster rate. **Sprint, plyometric, strength, and ballistic training are the most effective ways to increase stride rate and frequency.*

Agility is the ability to move rapidly while changing direction in response to a stimulus. Agility requires several complex systems and components including *mobility, coordination, balance, power, SSC efficiency, stabilization, proper technique, strength, flexibility, body control, footwork, rapid ability to accelerate and decelerate, anticipation, and scanning ability.*

Agility drills include multiple movements such as *linear sprints, backpedaling, side shuffling, drop-stepping, cariocas, cutting, pivoting, jumps, and cross-overs.* **The T-Test and pro-agility test (20-yard shuttle) are two of the most common agility assessments.*

Speed and Agility Drills

Form drills are used to improve technique and serve as a general warm-up. Exercises include *arm swings, butt kicks, high knees, ankling, marching, and pawing.*

Linear sprints: Short *(10 – 20 yards)* / Moderate *(40 – 60 yards)* / Long *(>60 yards)*

Overspeed training: allows the client to attain supramaximal speed *(by increasing stride length and frequency)*, or an assisted speed that is greater than maximal effort. **Downhill running, towing, and high-speed treadmill running can be used for overspeed training.*

Resisted sprint training: Involves the client sprinting maximally against resistance. **Wind (headwind), sleds, speed chutes, bands, sand, weighted vests, harnesses, partner, stairs, and hills can be used for resistance.*

Programmed agility drills: Preplanned drills where the client is aware of the movements prior to beginning the drill. **T-Test, pro agility, 505 agility, figure-8 drill, and right triangle drill are some examples.*

Reactive agility drills: The client must react to a stimulus. **Examples include box jump with multidirectional sprint, partner shadow / mirror drills, slap or tag drills, and drills that involve ball tossing and catching.*

Quickness agility drills: Designed to produce fast movements and quick feet. **Examples include agility ladder drills, pop-up drills (from the ground), down-and-up drills (sprawl in wrestling, burpee), and the resisted let-go.*

T-Test: The test begins with the client standing at cone A once T-test layout is set up *(see below)* and athlete has warmed up. The client then sprints toward cone B on an auditory signal to start touching the base of cone B with the right hand. Then while facing forward and not crossing the feet, they shuffle to the left 5 yards touching the base of cone C with the left hand. The client then shuffles to the right 10 yards touching the base of cone D with their right hand. The client then shuffles to the left 5 yards touching the base of cone B with their left hand and next runs backward crossing point A where the time is stopped. *The best time of (2) trials / attempts is recorded to the nearest 0.1 seconds.*

Failure to do the following results in disqualification of an attempt: The individual must face forward the entire time while not crossing the feet during shuffling movements. They must also touch the base of each cone except for the final backward run past point A.

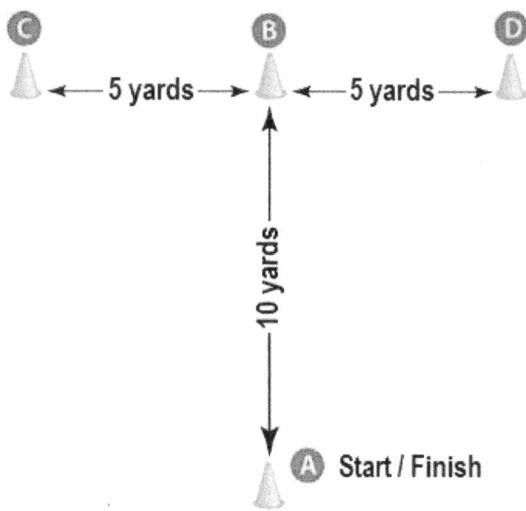

Pro Agility Test: The client begins by straddling the center most line in a three-point stance. On an auditory signal they sprint 5 yards to the line on their left, then change direction and sprint 10 yards to the line on the right, then again changes direction and sprints 5 yards to the left back to the center line. **Hand or foot contact must be made with all indicated lines and repeated the same way during the second trial.** *The best time of (2) trials / attempts is recorded to the nearest 0.01 seconds.*

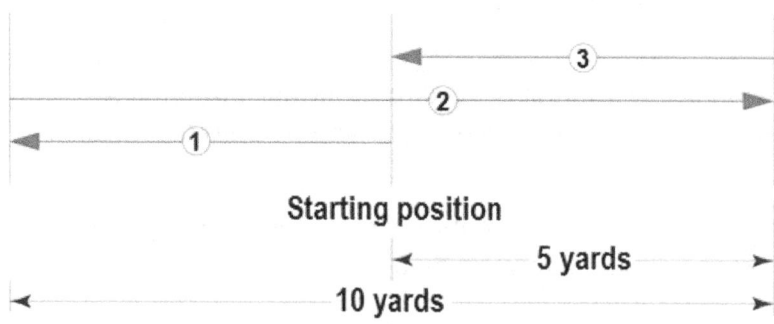

Programming for Children

Children and adolescents include individuals from 6 – 17 years of age. ACSM recommends **children participate in at least 60 minutes of moderate to vigorous intensity physical activity** per day. Including resistance exercise and bone-loading activity on at least 3 days per week.

The (3) target areas when designing an exercise program for children include:
Aerobic endurance, Muscular strengthening, and Bone-strengthening activities.

Regular endurance, resistance, and bone-loading exercise will confer favorable training adaptations in children, resulting in benefits to cardiovascular, metabolic, and skeletal health.

Exercise programs for children should be age-appropriate and also include enjoyable activities for them to perform. **Keeping activity fun and safe is important when working with children.*

Resistance activity should be performed for *8 – 15 submaximal repetitions to moderate fatigue (performed with good technique).* Body weight or other resistance modalities can be used.

Programming for Clients with CVD

According to the American Heart Association, more than 1 in 3 Americans have one or more types of Cardiovascular Disease (CVD). Each one metabolic equivalent (MET) increase in cardiorespiratory fitness can reduce the risk of CVD and all-cause mortality by 8% - 17%.

For most previously sedentary clients with CVD, the **threshold intensity** for improving cardiorespiratory fitness approximates to **40% - 80% of VO$_2$R or HRR (Heart Rate Reserve).**

Energy expenditure requirements are **1,000 kcal per week** to modify risk factors. This can be accomplished with **moderate-intensity exercise on 5 – 7 days per week for 20 – 60 minutes per session.** Progression should aim towards the upper end of total weekly energy expenditure recommendations at 3,000 kcal per week.

Resistance training programs should have the following two primary goals for clients with CVD:

1) To maintain and improve muscular fitness levels for performing activities of daily living.
2) To reduce the cardiovascular demands associated with performing these tasks.

Resistance training should occur on **2 – 3 nonconsecutive days per week**. Sessions composed of **8-10 exercises** are recommended for **one set of 10-15 repetitions** *(initially until multiple sets can be tolerated)* to moderate fatigue *(RPE range of 11- 13 / light to somewhat hard).*

*Isometric exercises, tight gripping of weight handles/bars, straining, holding breath, and the Valsalva maneuver should all be avoided for clients with CVD.

Programming for Older Adults

The functional capacity of the average sedentary person declines by 30% between the ages of 30 and 70 years. Being regularly active throughout life not only significantly minimizes the normal age-related changes but also restores functional capacity in previously sedentary adults.

Anaerobic, aerobic, and resistance-training exercise programs can increase aerobic capacity and muscular strength by 20%-30% or more, respectively, in older adults. These adaptations can occur at least into an individual's 70's. *Regular involvement in aerobic, anaerobic, resistance, flexibility, and functional training are key factors of successful aging.*

Personal Trainers should design programs for older adults to support *"successful aging"* with the following (3) primary goals in mind:

1) Prevent or delay the progression of chronic diseases *(and/or possibly "reverse" symptoms as in normalizing blood glucose)*
2) Maintain or enhance cardiorespiratory fitness levels *(functional capacity).*
3) Prevent functional limitations and disabilities.

Exercise intensity for older adults can be measured on a 0 – 10 scale with 0 equivalent to sitting and 10 being maximal effort. Moderate-intensity activity would be a 5 or 6 and vigorous-intensity activity at a 7 or 8.

Moderate-intensity activity: A minimum of 30 minutes per day *(greater benefits up to 60 min per day)* on at least 5 days per week. *(150 – 300 minutes per week total).*

Vigorous-intensity activity: 20 – 30 minutes per day on at least 3 days per week *(for those who are interested and able)*. *(75 – 100 minutes per week total).* *Exercise can be accumulated in 10-minute bouts if not performed continuously.*

Resistance training should be performed at 60% - 70% of 1RM *(if known)* or use the 0 – 10 point intensity scale for moderate to vigorous exercise. *ACSM recommends 8-10 exercises be performed for one set of 10-15 repetitions during resistance training sessions for older adults.*

Poor flexibility and decreased strength have been associated with a diminished ability to perform activities of daily living (ADL). *Older adults should perform flexibility training at least 2 days per week.* Static stretching should only be performed when the muscles are warm and ideally at the end of a cardiorespiratory and/or resistance training session.

Balance training is important to add to older adults exercise programs to help decrease the risks of falls commonly seen in the older population and improve their functional abilities. *Both static and dynamic balance activities may be performed 3 days per week for 10 – 15 minutes per session.* Balance training can be integrated into various phases of a training session including the warm-up, main component, or cool-down.

*Balance exercises and training progression for older adults can be found in Table 20.6 and Figures 20.1 – 20.3 on Pages 558 & 559 of ACSM's Resources for the Personal Trainer - Fifth Edition.

Programming During Pregnancy and Postpartum

Pregnancy requires an additional intake of 300 kcal per day *(approximately)* to fulfill the increased metabolic demands of pregnancy.

Warning signs to terminate exercise during pregnancy include *vaginal bleeding, amniotic fluid leakage, dyspnea prior to exertion, dizziness, chest pain, headache, calf pain or swelling, and muscle weakness affecting balance.*

After the first trimester exercises in the supine position should be avoided due to the potential obstruction of venous return and subsequent risk of orthostatic hypotension.

*Isometric and heavy resistance exercise is not recommended during pregnancy.

Programming for Clients with Diabetes

Type 1 Diabetes occurs when pancreatic β-cells that produce insulin are destroyed by an autoimmune disorder, creating an absolute insulin deficiency *(no insulin production)* in the body.

Type 2 Diabetes occurs when insulin becomes ineffective at controlling blood glucose due to insulin resistance in body tissues. The pancreas increases insulin production in an attempt to overcome this resistance, causing an excess of blood insulin. Hyperinsulinemia *(elevated blood insulin)* can contribute to a host of problems over time including *hypertension, hypercholesterolemia, excessive blood clotting, atherosclerosis, and kidney stones.*

The main goal in the management of diabetes is to control blood glucose levels. **Normal resting blood glucose levels are 100 mg or less.** Diabetes is diagnosed typically when fasting blood glucose is **126 mg or greater on two or more occasions.** Diabetes prevention is appropriate for all populations, not only for the obese but also for older adults and at-risk children.

Hemoglobin A1c (HbA1C) is a measure of blood glucose control over the last 2 – 3 months. Normal ranges are between 3.5% and 5.5% for those without diabetes. A goal level for most people with diabetes is under 7%.

Programming Goals for those with Diabetes

1) Improve insulin sensitivity, blood glucose control, and decrease insulin requirements.
2) Improve cardiorespiratory fitness.
3) Improve blood lipid profiles.
4) Reduce blood pressure.
5) Improve muscular strength and endurance through enhancing skeletal muscle mass.
6) Improve flexibility and joint ROM.
7) Reduce body weight *(particularly intra-abdominal fat).*
8) Assist with decreasing the risk of diabetic complications.

Aerobic training is recommended **3 – 7 days per week for 20 – 60 minutes a day** *(can be accumulated with 10-minute bouts)* with no more than 2 consecutive days between sessions. *(150 minutes per week minimum).* Progressing to 5 days per week or even daily provides the most benefit for obese clients or those taking insulin. ***Consistency in a daily routine is a key factor in diabetes care.***

Exercise intensity ranges of **40% - 59% of VO$_2$R or HRR (Heart Rate Reserve)** are recommended for clients with diabetes. **RPE range of 11- 13 / light to somewhat hard*. Intensity should be adjusted based on the individual's health status and fitness capacity.

Resistance training to maintain muscle mass helps with managing and improving glycemic control and insulin sensitivity, decreasing HbA1C levels, reducing intra-abdominal fat, and improving the overall metabolic profile and quality of life for those with diabetes.

Clients with diabetes should check their blood glucose levels prior to exercise and ideally be in the range of 100 – 250 mg. If they are lower than this, they should eat a carbohydrate-rich snack to bring their levels up.

Hypoglycemia *(low blood glucose levels)* is one of the most common and potentially serious complications that can occur during or after exercise in individuals with diabetes. It is advised to have fruit juice or candy available if blood glucose gets too low.

Signs and Symptoms of Hyperglycemia and Hypoglycemia	
Hyperglycemia (>300 mg)	*Hypoglycemia (<70 mg or rapid drop in glucose)*
Dry Skin	Dizziness and headache
Hunger	Weakness and fatigue
Nausea / vomiting	Shaking
Blurred vision	Tachycardia *(fast heart rate)*
Frequent urination	Irritable
Extreme thirst	Confusion
Drowsiness	Sweating
Acetone breath *(fruity breath)*	Slurred speech
	Anxious
	Hunger

Programming for Obese Clients

Obesity is currently defined as having a BMI greater than 30.

Programming Goals for Obese Individuals
1) Maximize caloric expenditure.
2) Maintain or increase lean body mass to maintain resting metabolic rate.
3) Improve metabolic profile.
4) Lower the risk of comorbidities *(hypertension, diabetes, orthopedic problems)*.
5) Lower mortality risk.
6) Promote appetite control.
7) Improve mood state.

ACSM recommends a **minimum of 150 minutes per week of moderate-intensity** exercise for overweight and obese individuals.

Greater weight loss and prevention of weight regained is associated with higher doses of **250 – 300 minutes of moderate-intensity activity or approximately 2,000 kcal per week.**

Training frequency of 5 or more days per week is recommended to maximize energy expenditure. Starting with **30 minutes per day and gradually progressing to 60 minutes** is recommended. *Very deconditioned clients can begin with multiple bouts of 10 minutes or more and progress from there as conditioning improves.*

Exercise intensity ranges of **40% - 59% of VO$_2$R or HRR (Heart Rate Reserve)** are recommended for obese clients. *RPE range of 11- 13 / light to somewhat hard*. Intensity should be adjusted based on the individual's health status and fitness capacity.

Most evidence indicates that **exercise alone *(without dietary restriction)*** is fairly ineffective for weight loss with an average **of less than 3% reduction in weight**. Expectations and reality are often not aligned with both obese clients and Personal Trainers. Exercise alone should not be viewed as a quick fix for weight loss. Many lifestyle factors need to be addressed in order to lose weight and maintain that weight loss successfully. There is no singularly appropriate weight-loss treatment plan for all obese people.

It is important to note that health improvements are seen with regular physical activity regardless of how much weight the individual loses. Overall health should be encouraged as a driving factor for exercise along with weight loss goals.

Resistance training has been shown to improve *blood cholesterol improve insulin sensitivity, reduce glucose-stimulated plasma insulin concentrations, and improve systolic and diastolic blood pressure.* Resistance training may also improve the maintenance of lean body mass in clients following a calorically restricted diet.

Recommendations for Weight-Loss Programs

- Gradual weight loss of 1kg *(2.2 lbs)* or less per week.
- Daily, negative caloric balance should not exceed 500 – 1,000 kcal.
- Goal for long-term weight loss of at least 5% - 10% of total weight.
- Employ behavioral modification strategies to enhance adherence.
- Dietary intake should not be <1,200 kcal.
- Balanced diet with fat intake <30% of total calories consumed.

Programming for Clients with Hypertension

Hypertension *(high blood pressure)* is the most prevalent risk factor for CVD in the United States with 76.4 million adults *(about 1 in 3)* with hypertension. Hypertension is often called the *"silent killer"* due to the lack of signs or symptoms of the disease until the development of serious problems.

Hypertension is defined as an elevated systolic and/or diastolic blood pressure that meets or exceeds 140/90 mm Hg at rest.

Prehypertension is defined as an elevated systolic blood pressure between 120 – 139 mm Hg and/or diastolic between 80 – 90 mm Hg.

Exercise should be avoided if resting blood pressure exceeds 200/110 mm Hg and exercise terminated if blood pressure exceeds 220/115 mm Hg or the client experiences a 10 mm Hg drop in systolic blood pressure during exercise. **Hypertensive clients should also avoid isometric muscle contractions as these can cause large increases in blood pressure.*

Programming Goals for Hypertension

1) Lower systolic and diastolic blood pressures at rest and during exercise.
2) Lower the risk of mortality from CVD *(myocardial infarction(heart attack), stroke, heart failure, etc.)*
3) Lower the risk of other comorbidities *(kidney disease, eye problems, diabetes, etc.)*
4) Incorporate opportunities for clients to pursue other lifestyle changes *(stress management, diet, smoking cessation, weight management, etc.)*

Aerobic training variables *(Frequency, Intensity, Time, Type)* are the same as recommendations mentioned for obese individuals.

Resistance training is considered a supplement to aerobic exercise and should not be prescribed as the primary form of activity for clients with hypertension. When supplementing with resistance training, *intensity should be kept at 60% - 80% of 1RM.*

Hypertension is often associated with a variety of conditions that may require special attention and specific precautions during exercise.

Programming for Clients with Comorbidities

Comorbidity refers to the simultaneous presence of two chronic diseases or conditions.

Approximately 80% of individuals aged 65 years or older are living with at least one chronic health problem, and 50% are living with two chronic conditions.

Sedentary lifestyle is a controllable risk factor for many chronic health conditions.

Programming Goals for Clients with Comorbidities

1) Lower the overall risk of mortality by identifying the condition with the highest mortality risk and prioritizing exercise program design around this condition.

2) Recognize that the presence of comorbidities may serve as competing demands on client's self-management resources, thus reducing time and energy an individual has remaining to devote to each and every condition. These individuals will require additional guidance and resources provided by the personal trainer to ensure that all conditions are managed effectively.

3) Have realistic expectations for improvement for all comorbidities. Improvement is not always feasible, and there will be instances where maintaining functional capacity or stabilizing the disease process can and should be viewed as a successful outcome.

Aerobic Exercise Prescription for Common Clinical Populations

Condition	Frequency (days per week)	Intensity (VO_2R or HRR)	Time (minutes per day)
Arthritis	3 – 5	40% – 59%	20 – 30
Cardiac Disease	3 – 7	40% – 80%	20 – 60
Dyslipidemia	≥ 5	40% – 75%	30 – 60
Hypertension	Most if not all	40% – 59%	30 – 60
Obesity	≥ 5	40% – 59% (potential progression to ≥ 60%)	30 – 60
Osteoporosis	4 – 5	40% – 59%	30 – 60
Type 2 Diabetes	3 – 7	40% – 59% (≥ 60% for those already active)	20 – 60

Although experienced Personal Trainers can work with clients with stable chronic disease who are able to exercise independently, it is important to recognize situations when consultation with medical personnel is necessary and/or when the Personal Trainer should not undertake a client.

Domain III: Exercise Leadership and Client Education

The following areas are covered in this domain:

- Customer Service and Hospitality
- Building Rapport
- Nonverbal Communication Skills
- Personal Trainer Tool Kit
- Coaching Techniques
- Types of Learners
- Types of Feedback
- Client Feedback
- Behavior Change Strategies
- Adherence to Exercise
- Overcoming Barriers
- Nutrition and Human Performance
- Fluid and Hydration
- Supplements
- Weight Loss
- The Female Athlete Triad

Customer Service and Hospitality

Optimal client care and effective customer service are the primary responsibilities of every Personal Trainer. Each person that a trainer comes in contact with throughout their work day *(who is not on staff)* is a potential customer. Below is a checklist of customer service skills all Personal Trainers should have and continually work to improve.

- Client safety
- Courtesy call 24-48 hours prior to meeting.
- Respond to phone, text, and e-mail messages promptly and courteously.
- Demonstrate organization and reliability and always follow up on what has been promised.
- Plan each workout *(Provide fitness training programs that are based on science or credible sources.)*
- Answer client's questions concisely and accurately within the scope of practice.
- Refer clients to appropriate professionals when the issue is outside the scope of practice.
- Maintain a professional appearance *(Dress appropriately and professionally)*
- Greeting and punctuality *(Be on time, or early, for appointments)*
- Utilize proper charting
- Be attentive
- Listen to the client concerns, respond with sincerity, and solicit feedback.
- Speak respectfully to the client and of others.
- Innovation and problem-solving skills
- Maintain professional conduct in the training facility
- Help keep the facility clean
- Work on self-improvement

Characteristics of hospitality include the following:

- *Optimistic warmth*: Genuine kindness, thoughtfulness, and a sense that the glass is always half full.
- *Intelligence*: Open-mindedness and an insatiable curiosity to learn.
- *Work ethic*: A natural tendency to do something as well as possible.
- *Empathy*: An awareness of, care for, and connection to how others feel and how the individual's actions affect others.
- *Self-awareness and Integrity*: Understanding what makes a person tick and a natural inclination to be accountable for doing the right thing.

Examples of hospitality include the following:

- Greet the client with an appropriately firm handshake, authentic smile, and eye contact.
- Convey that the client's best interest is in mind under any circumstance.
- Address client requests and do what is possible to make them happen.
- At the end of a session, sincerely thank the client for his or her time.
- Make follow-up calls/e-mails to see how the client feels after a personal training session.
- Send a handwritten card to thank the client after an initial appointment or when a significant goal has been reached.
- Search for opportunities to go above and beyond what is expected.

Building Rapport

Rapport refers to a sense of trust, respect, and/or confidence, which a client holds for their Personal Trainer. Rapport begins with the initial first impressions a client has and continues to develop through the use of good verbal and nonverbal communication. A personal trainer should possess excellent communication and teaching skills to create a climate of trust and respect with the client. Look to find common ground with clients so that conversation flows easily. Expressing **empathy, warmth, and genuineness** are three attributes to building a successful client-trainer relationship. Anticipating the client's needs shows attention to detail and helps to build rapport. **Clients will not care how much you know until they know how much you care.** Future teachings and valuable information that a personal trainer has to share will go unheard if they have not built this foundation of mutual understanding, trust, and respect with their clients. **Positive first impressions are the foundation for the rapport-building process.*

Tips for Building Rapport:

- Be sure to display / communicate your credentials.
- Confirm your professionalism by dressing and acting professionally.
- Highlight things that you have in common such as likes, dislikes, or experiences *(find common ground to show you relate to each other)*.
- Affirm any client strengths that you have noted *(positive feedback)*.
- Empathize with their struggles / feelings.
- Self-disclosure: *Share relevant struggles you have had in the past, take a sincere interest in your client – people can detect insincerity.*
- Nonverbal cues: *Have good eye contact, open posture, and appropriate facial expressions.*
- Remain non-judgmental and open-minded.
- Be a mindful and active listener and remain present in the moment.
- Offer explanations for the components of intervention
- Speak calmly and confidently.
- Continuously ask your client how they feel about the information you are providing them throughout the session.

Earn and keep the trust of clients by expressing the following behaviors: *Dependability, Integrity, and Empathy.*

Maintain credibility by being a *positive role model* who is *honest and consistent.*

Relationship marketing states that a personal relationship with the customer should take precedence, and sale will follow. Retaining existing clients should take precedence over seeking new customers. Loyal customers will spread the word about your business by word-of-mouth advertising.

Nonverbal Communication Skills *(Body Language)*

- *Appearance and physique*: Maintain good hygiene along with a healthy and fit appearance.
- *Eye contact*: The more frequent eye contact the better, although avoid staring for more than a few seconds at a time. This can make the client uncomfortable and may be construed as flirtatious.
- *Facial expressions*: Smile often and appear interested.
- *Head movements*: Keep chin up and nod *"yes"* to show interest.
- *Gestures*: Be expressive with hands and body movements without exaggeration.
- *Posture*: Sit and stand erect and lean forward to show interest. Keep arms and legs uncrossed to convey a secure and welcoming demeanor.
- *Proximity and orientation*: Be as close as possible without crowding the client. A comfortable range is between 1.5 & 4ft. Read the client's body language and adjust accordingly.
- *Timing and synchronization*: Speed up activities but not to the point of ineffectiveness.
- *Nonverbal aspects of speech*: Balance the need to listen with the need to speak

*Expressing enthusiasm can lead to all of the behaviors mentioned above without consciously focusing on each one.

Personal Trainer Tool Kit

- Effective communication skills *(in-person, phone, and written such as an e-mail)*
- Ability to motivate appropriately
- Ability to influence behavior change
- Effective interviewing and screening
- Effective use of goals and objectives
- Effective and safe exercise program design
- Ability to demonstrate, instruct, spot, and supervise appropriate exercise movements
- Effective use of up-to-date technology in order to obtain continuing educational opportunities via webinars and other online resources
- Obtaining new primary or specialty certification skills
- Effective use of social networking sites, Web sites, blogs, e-mail blasts, and so on for marketing and monitoring purposes
- Using a sound business model

Coaching Techniques

Active Listening: Active listening involves nodding, making eye contact, and restating important information the client has stated. Be nonjudgmental and open-minded. Give verbal and nonverbal feedback to indicate attention and understanding. Make sure to receive affirmation from the client on feedback given. Identify statements that indicate a teaching and/or learning opportunity. **There are (4) Elements of Active Listening**:

- Listening to the spoken statements of the client.
- Observing nonverbal communication.
- Listening to the context of the clients' apprehensions.
- Listening to the context of the clients' statements that may need to be challenged.

Empathy: Match the client's emotions to show affective empathy. The ability to identify with their perspective shows an understanding that helps to develop trust and rapport. Being honest, demonstrating effective communication, showing mutual respect, and warm responsiveness to the client are all qualities of an empathetic person.
"Seek first to understand, and then to be understood." – Stephen Covey

Motivational Interviewing (MI): Helps a client commit to changing unhealthy behavior by combining empathetic counseling and a direct approach to decisive change. Ask open-ended questions that require more than a *"yes"* or *"no"* answer. Encourage the client to talk about what needs to be changed & then help them find ways to elicit that behavior change. Personal trainers should empower their clients to take control, be independent, and self-sufficient with their exercise program. Teach and help them find enjoyment in the experience. Helping clients take ownership and control increases their intrinsic motivation. The overall goal of MI is to resolve any ambivalence *(mixed feelings)* from the client to encourage the client's *"change talk"* and reduce the amount of *"resistance talk."*

*A personal trainer should not try to control or manipulate a client into acting a certain way as this will diminish the intrinsic motivation of the client.

Positive Affirmation: Positive words promote positive attitudes and positive outcomes. Positive reinforcement helps the client to build self-esteem and motivation for exercise.

Client-centered approach: The motivational interviewing skills of rapport building, exhibiting empathy, and active listening are central to keeping the client's perspective at the forefront.

Giving **unsolicited advice** can hinder behavior change because it can be perceived as condescending and undermines the client's intelligence and sense of independence.

Types of Learners

Visual: Someone who learns through seeing images & techniques. Visual learners must first see what they are expected to know.

Auditory: A person who learns best through listening. They depend on hearing & speaking as a main way of learning.

Kinesthetic: This learning style requires that you manipulate or touch material to learn. It is often combined with auditory or visual learning techniques producing multi-sensory learning.

"Tell, Show, Do" *Tell me and I'll forget, Show me and I may remember, Involve me and I'll understand.* Trainers should keep this proverb in mind when teaching exercises to clients. Using a combination of *"Tell, Show, Do"* is the best practice when teaching. Starting with a brief and simple explanation *"Tell"* along with demonstration *"Show"* followed by the client performing the exercise *"Do"* The personal trainer should observe the client while they perform the exercise and prepare to provide helpful feedback.

Types of Feedback

Evaluative: A summary for the client of how well they have performed a given task.
e.g. "You maintained great form & control during that set."

Supportive: Encourage the client when they perform a task properly. This type of feedback is motivational for the client & helps them adhere to the exercise program.
e.g. "Great job on that last set! Way to finish strong!"

Descriptive: Specific information that helps the client understand what they need to do in order to improve.
e.g. "Make sure to keep your core tight & back straight during the deadlift to protect from injury."

*The type of feedback that provides information on progress can be referred to as ***knowledge of results***.

Client Feedback

Seeking client feedback will help the personal trainer ensure client satisfaction and enjoyment of the program. Paying attention to both verbal and nonverbal feedback will assist the trainer in properly progressing and modifying the clients training program as needed to achieve their goals. Scheduling periodic program evaluations and goal reviews will also ensure client expectations are met.

Behavior Change Strategies

Appreciative Inquiry (AI): Focuses on exploring and amplifying the strengths of the client. AI has **5 phases of Development**:

- *Define* strengths and what is to be learned about the process.
- *Discover* what may work best.
- *Dream* of how the plan will work.
- *Design* a plan with the client.
- *Deliver* the plan using both short-term and long-term goals.

The 5 A's model of Behavior Change: An evidence-based approach used to change a variety of less than desirable health behaviors.

- *Assessing* the client's beliefs, behaviors, and motivations.
- *Advising* the client based on health risks and behaviors.
- *Agreeing* on realistic short-term and long-term goals.
- *Assisting* the client with anticipating barriers and developing a specific plan.
- *Arranging* sessions with a client as a method of support.

*An example of the 5 A's model is given in Box 9.10 on Page 261 of ACSM's Resources for the Personal Trainer - Fifth Edition.

Transtheoretical Model (TTM)

The TTM Model is composed of these four components: *Stages of change, Processes of change, Self-efficacy, and Decisional balance.*

Stages of Change

- **Pre-contemplation**: The client is not intending to take action toward change and is not considering the benefits of change at this time.

- **Contemplation**: The client is considering the negative consequences of their behavior and is considering changes within the next 6 months.

- **Preparation**: The client has developed a plan of action toward behavior change and will be making changes in the immediate future *(next 30 days)*.

- **Action**: The client is actively making behavior changes *(regularly active for **less than 6 months**).*

- **Maintenance**: The client has been actively maintaining the changes made during the action stage, the new behaviors have been established for **6 months or more**, and the client is now working to prevent relapse.

*See Figure 7.2 on Page 204 of ACSM's Resources for the Personal Trainer - Fifth Edition.
*Know how to determine what stage of change the client is in based on their responses during motivational interviewing.

Process of change involves using interventions specific to a client's current stage of change to help them transition to the next stage of change. This will help increase the success of the client adopting a new behavior. There are **10 process of change** that includes both cognitive and behavioral strategies to implement during various stages of change. **See Table 7.1 on Page 205 of ACSM's Resources for the Personal Trainer - Fifth Edition.*

Self-Efficacy: The belief in one's own capabilities to successfully engage in a physical-activity program along with one's ability for self-management, goal achievement & effectiveness.

Self-Efficacy is developed through the following six sources of information: *Past performance experience, Vicarious experience, Verbal persuasion, Physiological state appraisals, Emotional state and mood appraisals, and Imaginal experiences.*

Decisional Balance involves the perceived *"pros"* and *"cons"* one has about adopting and/or maintaining behavior change. The client must come to this conclusion themselves to take ownership of their goal and not feel forced into change by the personal trainer. The personal trainer should also acknowledge the challenges *(cons)* the client presents. This shows the trainer has an understanding and empathy for their situation which builds the clients trust in the trainer and likelihood for change *(builds rapport)*.

Health Belief Model (HBM)

The perceived threat of a potential health problem or susceptibility to potential health consequences & the belief that making suggested behavioral changes will result in a decreased risk of those consequences.

Example would be a sedentary person who has high blood pressure that decides to regularly exercise & eat better to decrease their blood pressure naturally. They must believe that making those behavioral changes will decrease the health risk associated with high blood pressure.

Health Belief Model (HBM) Constructs and Strategies can be found in Table 7.2 on Page 209 of ACSM's Resources for the Personal Trainer - Fifth Edition.

Theory of Planned Behavior (TPB)

TPB suggests that the intention to engage in a behavior will ultimately result in that behavior.

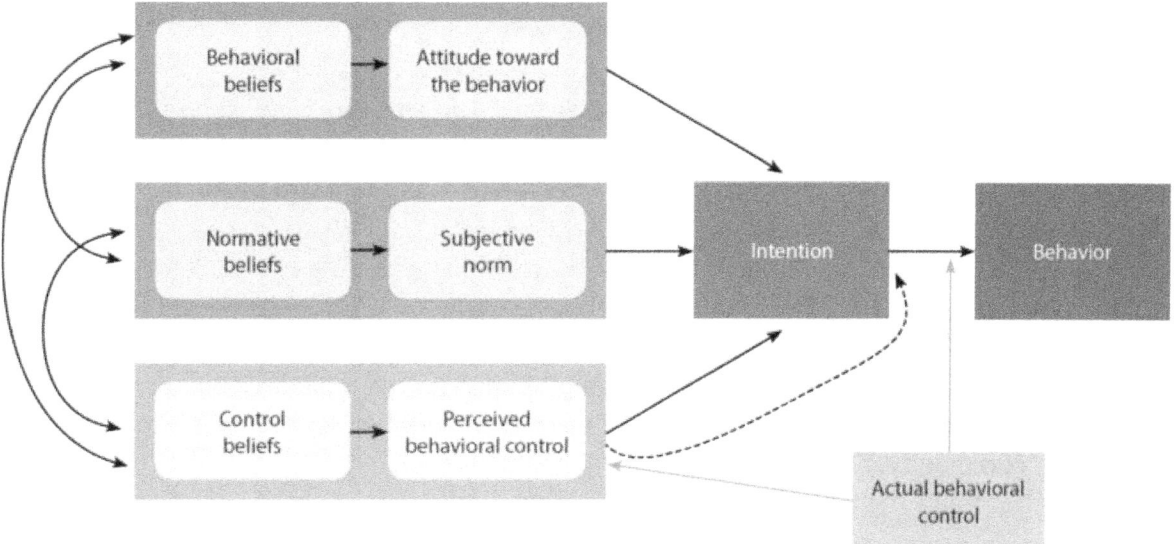

Social Cognitive Theory (SCT)

This theory states that outcome expectations & self-efficacy *(situation specific self-confidence)* are the most important factors in behavior change. SCT emphasizes client's thoughts & feelings to empower them to make decisions & behavior change.

The basis of SCT along with thoughts, feelings, and behaviors can be found in Figures 7.5 & 7.6 on Page 212 of ACSM's Resources for the Personal Trainer - Fifth Edition.

For comparison of the strengths and limitations for all of the Behavior-Change Theories see Table 7.3 on Pages 219 & 220 of ACSM's Resources for the Personal Trainer - Fifth Edition.

Goal Setting Theory (GST)

SMART Goals: *Specific, Measurable, Attainable (action-oriented), Relevant, Time-Bound*

A **Process goal** is a goal a person achieves by doing something *(the process)*, such as completing a certain number of workouts each week. A **Product goal** is something that is achieved *(the product)* such as weight loss or an increase in strength. The following four mechanisms play a role in goal-related behavior change:

- Goals direct attention toward desired behaviors
- Goals lead to greater effort
- Goals extend the time and energy devoted to a desired behavior
- Goals increase the use of goal-relevant skills

Small Changes Model (SCM)

The belief of this model is that clients will maintain smaller behavior changes more easily and will continue to build upon them over time.

SMALL Goals: *Self-selected, Measurable, Action-oriented, Linked to your life, Long-term*

*The Small Changes Model (SCM) can be found in Figure 7.7 on Page 215 of ACSM's Resources for the Personal Trainer - Fifth Edition.

Socioecological Model (SEM)

This model states that health behaviors are not only shaped by the individual but also environmental influences. Behaviors are shaped by interpersonal interactions, the surrounding environment, community, and policy.

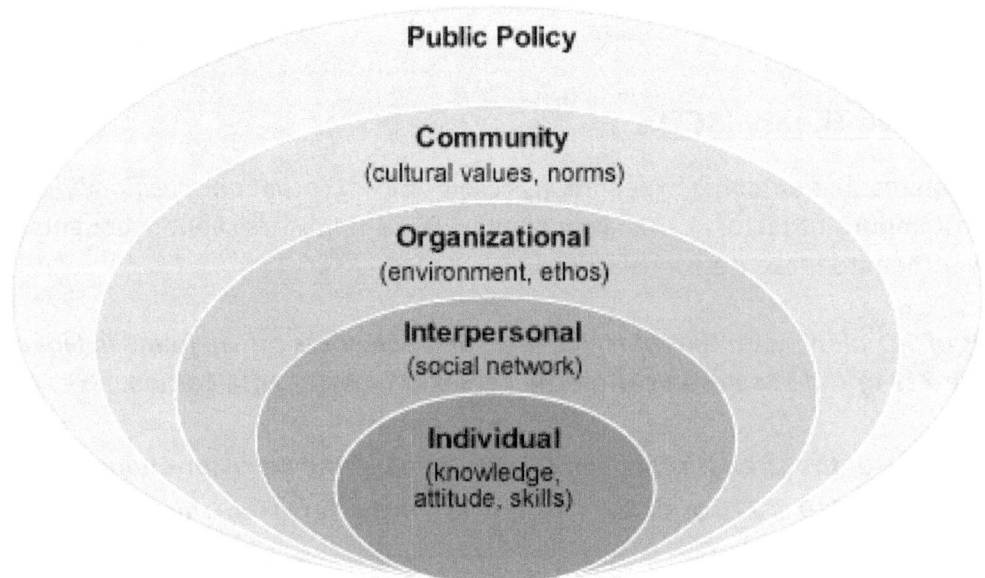

Adherence to Exercise

- It takes about 6 months of regular exercise to see lasting health benefits.
- 50% of people who begin an exercise program quit within 6 months.
- Involving clients in the planning stage of an exercise program by asking for their input and working together to design the program helps them take responsibility *(autonomy)* for the program and increases exercise adherence.
- An individual who perceives that the benefits of exercise outweigh the barriers to exercise is more likely to adhere to an exercise program.
- Helping clients achieve their own *self-regulation* for exercise is necessary to increase exercise adherence. Self-regulation strategies include planning exercise, setting exercise-related goals, self-monitoring exercise behavior & avoiding relapse.

Top 3 theory-based concepts related to exercise adherence: *Self-efficacy, Motivation (for exercise), and Self-worth.*

Self-Efficacy: The belief in one's own capabilities to successfully engage in a physical-activity program along with one's ability for self-management, goal achievement & effectiveness.

Self-Worth: Satisfaction individuals have with themselves.

Self-Concept: Perceived worthiness, capabilities, or skills of one's self-based on inner belief and the responses of others.

Self-Esteem: Confidence in one's self-worth or abilities.

Self-Monitoring refers to the practice of tracking one's own behavior for the dual purpose of increasing awareness and monitoring progress.

Self-Regulation: Strategies for planning, organizing, and managing exercise activities to *"stay on track."*

*Notice that all of these terms begin with *"Self"* which suggests that **adherence to exercise needs to come from** *"within"* **the individual** *(client).* Personal Trainers should understand their clients perceived barriers to exercise through active listening. Once the barriers are identified the personal trainer should equip their clients with the appropriate strategies and skills to maintain adherence.

Continuing self-regulation, intrinsic motivation along with setting achievable goals will help a client's self-efficacy and prevention of relapse.

__See factors related to adherence Table 8.1 on Page 231 of ACSM's Resources for the Personal Trainer - Fifth Edition.__

Innovative Strategies to Increase Adherence

Extrinsic Motivation: Participation in exercise to achieve external outcomes such as weight loss and appearance. Extrinsic motivation is good for short-term SMALL goals. External motivation from trainer should inspire intrinsic motivation of the client.

Intrinsic Motivation: Participation in exercise to achieve internal outcomes such as enjoyment of exercise itself or the sense of accomplishment after the workout is completed. Intrinsic motivation for exercise is better for lifelong adherence to exercise.

Self-Determination Theory (SDT): Suggests that the following psychological needs have to be satisfied in order to internalize extrinsic motivation and become intrinsically motivated.

- **Autonomy**: The desire to be responsible for choosing the behavior in which you participate.
- **Relatedness**: The desire to connected with others and feel understood by others.
- **Competence**: The belief that you are able to complete a specific behavior in order to reach your goal.

The personal trainer can use the internet for online coaching of clients and to provide additional support for clients, video demonstrations of exercises, online self-monitoring tools, and newsletters. Personal Trainers are encouraged to creatively utilize innovations in Internet technology to help their clients adhere to exercise.

Other methods of communication include phone calls, print materials, e-mail, and other Web-based materials. These forms of communication may be helpful when face-to-face meetings are not convenient or possible.

Personal Trainers can encourage clients to utilize the physical environment with the following strategies: *actively commuting to work, cycling/walking to complete errands or when visiting friends; or parking farther away, using the stairs, and taking walking breaks at work*

Exercising outdoors in the natural environment is another great way to improve mental well-being and motivation for exercise.

Overcoming Barriers

Factors influencing exercise participation & adherence: Personal Attributes *(Demographic Variables, Health Status, Activity History, Psychological Traits, Knowledge, Attitudes, and Beliefs)* Environmental Factors *(Access to Facilities, Time, and Social Support)* Physical-Activity Factors *(Intensity and Injury)*

Personal Barriers: These can be internal or behavioral such as lack of time, motivation, knowledge, injury & extrinsic motivation. Discussing strategies for time management, sharing information about the benefits of exercise & setting challenging but attainable goals can help increase a client's self-efficacy to overcome personal barriers.

Social Barriers: These barriers arise from within the client's social network *(close family & friends)*. Examples of social barriers include caregiving *(such as child care)*, lack of social support & sociocultural barriers. Understanding what types of social support a client needs & teaching them how to obtain that support may help them achieve the support required to adhere to exercise.

Social support has (4) types: *Emotional, Tangible, Informational, and Appraisal*

*Examples of each type of support can be found in Table 8.3 on Pages 244 of ACSM's Resources for the Personal Trainer - Fifth Edition.

Environmental Barriers: These are physical barriers that are often outside of an individual's control that prevent them from being active. Lack of access to exercise facilities, bad weather & safety concerns *(absence of sidewalks or bike lanes, crime)* are some examples. Providing clients with opportunities to be active outside of the gym, at their homes or within their daily lifestyles can help overcome lack of access.

*Strategies to overcome common barriers can be found in Table 8.2 on Pages 236 - 238 of ACSM's Resources for the Personal Trainer - Fifth Edition.

Avoiding Relapse: Psychological factors and high-risk situations such as life events *(births, deaths in the family)*, holidays, injuries, decreased social support and decreased motivation can impact continued adherence to exercise. These may cause a lapse *(brief period of two or more weeks)* or relapse *(complete return to sedentary behavior)* in exercise adherence. Discussing potential relapse situations before they occur with a client can prepare them to overcome and maintain their exercise routine. **Assertiveness** is an important characteristic for achieving success and avoiding relapse. The more assertive clients are with regard to their progress, concerns, accomplishments and struggles the more likely they are to achieve long-term success.

Nutrition and Human Performance

There are 6 classes of nutrients: Carbohydrates, Fats, Protein, Vitamins, Minerals & Water

Macronutrients: Carbohydrates, Fats & Protein *These are the energy sources for our body*

Micronutrients: Vitamins & Minerals

Fat soluble nutrients: Vitamins A, D, E & K

Water soluble nutrients: Vitamins B, C & Niacin

Minerals: Calcium, Phosphorus, Magnesium, Iron, Zinc, Copper, Selenium, Iodine, Fluoride, Chromium, Sodium, & Potassium

Nutrient density: The nutrient content of a food relative to its calories.

Kilocalorie (Calorie) Breakdown

Fat = 9 calories per gram
Protein = 4 calories per gram
Carbohydrates = 4 calories per gram
Alcohol = 7 calories per gram
3500 kcal (calories) = 1 pound of fat

Basal Metabolic Rate (BMR): Calories burned daily without movement.
To gain or lose weight one should increase or decrease calories by 300 to 400 kcals per day.

Daily Macronutrient Recommendations

Carbohydrates: (55% - 65% of total calories)
General population should have around 3 grams per kilogram of body weight per day, those that exercise more than an hour a day 4-5 g per kg, and high-intensity exercisers 8-12 g per kg
Most, if not all of carbohydrate intake should come from complex carbohydrates.

Protein: (10% - 35% of total calories)
0.8 grams per kilogram of body weight per day for the general population.
Adult athletes can range from 1.2 to 1.7 g per kg of body weight.

Fats: (20% to 35% of total calories)
Less than 10% of fat calories should come from saturated fat

Scope of Practice

Fitness professionals can and should share general nonmedical nutrition information with their clients. Fitness professionals can have informed discussions on nutrition with their clients but **never prescribe meal plans or supplements as it is outside of the scope of practice.**

Carbohydrates

Complex carbohydrate: A carbohydrate with more than 10 carbon/water units. Includes the fiber and starch found in whole grains and vegetables.

Simple carbohydrate: A carbohydrate with fewer than 10 carbon/water units. Includes glucose, sucrose, lactose, galactose maltose, and fructose.

Monosaccharides are made up of a singular sugar unit and include the following:

- *Glucose (blood sugar)*: A simple sugar manufactured by the body from carbohydrates, fat, and (to a lesser extent) protein that serves as the body's main source of fuel.
- *Fructose*: Known as the fruit sugar, found in fruits, honey, syrups, and certain vegetables.
- *Galactose (part of lactose)*: Combines with glucose and lactose.

Disaccharides are made up of two sugar units and include the following:

- *Sucrose (table sugar)*: A molecule made up of glucose and fructose.
- *Lactose*: A sugar present in milk that is composed of glucose and galactose.
- *Maltose*: Sugar produced in the breakdown of starch. Rare in our food supply.

High-fructose corn syrup (HFCS) is a sweetener made from cornstarch and converted to fructose in food processing.

Glucose is a simple sugar that is the preferred energy source for the human body. It is a compound of many carbohydrates. Some carbohydrates *(glucose)* are required for the oxidation *(burning)* of fat & also help keep protein *(muscle tissue)* from being broken down. However, too much glucose *(carbs/sugar)* causes an excessive insulin response that encourages the production of fat. **Glycemic index** is a measure of how carbohydrates affect blood sugar levels. Low glycemic foods help maintain glucose *(blood sugar)* levels that in turn maintains insulin balance which helps to keep the body out of the *"fat storing"* state. Blood glucose reaches peak an hour after a meal & returns to normal 2 hours after that, therefore eating every 2-4 hours helps avoid mental & muscle fatigue.

Glycogen is the storage form of glucose that is found in the liver & muscle tissues. When carbohydrate energy is needed, glycogen is converted into glucose for use by the muscle cells.

Dietary fiber is a carbohydrate that cannot be digested but aids in lowering fat & cholesterol absorption. Dietary fiber also improves blood sugar control. Since dietary fiber is non-digestible, it is subtracted from the total carbohydrate amount of a given food.

*If a food has 22 grams of total carbohydrates with 12 grams of dietary fiber then it has 10 grams of net carbs.

Fats

Lipids: A group of compounds that includes fatty acids, triglycerides *(fats and oils)*, phospholipids, and sterols such as cholesterol. Lipids are substances that are insoluble in water.

Saturated fat: A chain of carbons that are saturated with all of the hydrogens that it can hold; there are no double bonds.

Unsaturated fatty acids: Fatty acids that have areas that are not completely saturated with hydrogens, and therefore have double bonds where the hydrogen is missing.

Polyunsaturated: Fatty acids that have several spots where hydrogens are missing.
*Helps lower blood cholesterol levels

Monounsaturated: A fatty acid with just one missing hydrogen.
*Helps lower blood cholesterol levels while maintaining HDL

Consuming polyunsaturated & monounsaturated *"healthy fats"* along with regular exercise has been shown to improve lipid profiles. Regular exercise also helps to reduce LDL cholesterol.

Omega-3 fatty acids: Fatty acids that have anti-inflammatory effects and help to decrease blood clotting.

Omega-6 fatty acids: Fatty acids that promote blood clotting and cell membrane formation.

High-density lipoproteins (HDL): Carry lipids away from storage into the liver for metabolism and /or excretion. They are considered *"good cholesterol."*

Low-density lipoproteins (LDL): The major carrier of cholesterol & other lipids in the blood.
*Can accumulate on artery walls

Triglyceride: The chemical or substrate form in which most fat exists in food and in the body.

Long-chain fatty acids: Contains 14 or more carbon atoms

Medium-chain fatty acids: Contains 8-12 carbon atoms

*Medium chain triglycerides (MCT) are an excellent source of fuel for the body.

Short-chain fatty acids: Contains 6 or fewer carbon atoms

Protein

Protein: Long chains of amino acids linked by peptide bonds. Serve several essential functional roles in the body.

Complete protein: A protein that provides all of the essential amino acids in the amount the body needs and is also easy to digest and absorb; also called *high-quality protein*. *Found in meats, eggs, dairy products, hemp seeds, and the vegetable protein in soy.*

Incomplete protein: Food that does not contain all of the essential amino acids in the amount needed by the body. *Found in beans, legumes, grains, and vegetables.*

Complementary proteins: Consuming two or more incomplete proteins together to provide needed amino acids. *People who do not eat meat and dairy products can do this to get all of the essential amino acids.*

Humans are incapable of using protein for anabolic *(tissue building)* purposes above the level of 1.5 g per kg of body weight. Consuming a high-protein diet in excess of what the body can use for repair/building purposes will cause the kidneys to work harder to eliminate the increased urea produced.

Amino acids: The building blocks of proteins; composed of a central carbon atom, a hydrogen atom, an amino group, a carboxyl group, and an R-group.

There are **20 amino acids** found in the human body, **8 essential, 10 nonessential, and 2 semi-essential.**

The body cannot produce essential amino acids so they must be obtained from the foods we eat whereas nonessential amino acids can be produced by the body.

Semi-essential amino acids: Arginine and histidine are considered semi-essential because they cannot be manufactured by the body at a rate that will support growth *(especially in children)*.

Amino Acids		
Essential	**Nonessential**	**Semi-essential**
Isoleucine	Alanine	Arginine
Leucine	Asparagine	Histidine
Lysine	Aspartic acid	
Methionine	Cysteine	
Phenylalanine	Glutamic acid	
Threonine	Glutamine	
Tryptophan	Glycine	
Valine	Proline	
	Serine	
	Tyrosine	

Fluid and Hydration

About 60% of our total body weight is water. Most of the water in the human body (70%) is stored in the muscle tissues. Water helps to transport nutrients, rid the body of waste, regulate body temperature, lubricate joints, cushion vital organs, provides structure to the skin and body tissue.

Thirst sensation happens after 1 - 2 liters of fluid *(1% - 2% of body weight)* has been lost. In order to stay optimally hydrated during exercise, people should learn to consume fluids regularly or on a fixed time interval rather than relying on the thirst sensation. A good indicator of hydration is urine color. When optimally hydrated urine should be a near clear pale yellow, darker colored urine indicates a state of dehydration. Proper hydration during exercise produces the following benefits:

- A less pronounced increase in heart rate
- A less pronounced increase in core body temperature
- Improvement in cardiac stroke volume (SV) & cardiac output (Q)
- Improvement in skin blood flow *(enabling better sweat rates & improved cooling)*
- Maintenance of better blood volume
- A reduction in net muscle glycogen usage *(improving endurance)*

Dehydration affects the body's ability to cool itself with sweat and leads to overheating, often compounded with a severe loss of electrolytes. Severe dehydration can lead to heat stroke.

Signs of dehydration include the following: *Dry mouth, Dry skin, Headache, Rapid heartbeat, Rapid breathing, Fever, Thirst, Decreased urine output, Sleepiness or tiredness, Dizziness, Sunken eyes, Low blood pressure, Constipation, Delirium, and Unconsciousness.*

Insensible water loss is water lost through mild daily sweating and exhalation of air humidified by the lungs, as well as other minor water losses, such as secretions from the eyes, that generally go unnoticed.

*A 2% loss in body weight through dehydration is associated with reduced performance.

*Losses in excess of 5% of body weight can decrease the capacity for work by about 30%.

*Consuming fluids such as sports drinks with a 6% to 8% carbohydrate solution along with 100 – 200 mg of sodium per cup is ideal to help maintain hydration.

A simple way to estimate hydration levels is to measure changes in body weight from pre- to post workout or training session. **20 ounces *(600 mL)* of fluid should be consumed for each pound of body weight lost. Fluid should be consumed within 2 hours post-exercise or competition to replenish hydration to pre-exercise body weight.**

Electrolytes: Minerals in blood and other body fluids that carry an electrical charge. Minerals include *potassium, sodium, calcium, chloride, magnesium, and phosphate.* Sodium and potassium are the most important electrolytes depleted with sweat. They are commonly found in sports drinks to help replace what is lost during exercise. Electrolyte replacement is most important with prolonged physical activity. Sports drinks are ideal for those who exercise longer than 60 minutes.

Warning Signs of Dehydration, Heat Exhaustion, and Heat Stroke	
Warning Sign	*What to Do?*
Dehydration with loss of energy and performance	Drink carbohydrate- and electrolyte-containing sports drinks. Avoid beverages with carbonation, which can cause gastrointestinal distress.
Dehydration with muscle cramps	Immediately stop exercising and massage the cramping muscle(s). Consuming a sports drink that contains sodium may help relieve the cramp.
Heat exhaustion with dizziness, light-headedness, and cold, clammy skin	Immediately replace fluids while in a cool, shaded area until the dizziness passes. Stretching may improve circulation and prevent fainting. Lying with the legs elevated will improve blood circulation to the head, thereby alleviating the dizziness.
Heat exhaustion with nausea / headaches	Rest in a cool place until nausea passes. Drinking fluids to rehydrate is critical. Lying down may help relieve headaches.
Heat stroke with high body temperature and dry skin	Immediately get out of the heat and seek immediate medical treatment. Feeling chilly with arms tingling and with goosebumps means skin circulation has shut down and heat stroke is imminent. This is an extremely serious condition that must be immediately treated.
Heat stroke with confusion or unconsciousness	Confusion strongly suggests, and unconsciousness confirms heat stroke. This is a medical emergency that calls for fast cooling with ice baths or any other available means to lower body temperature.

Dietary Recommendations Before, During, and After Exercise or Competition

One day before a Competition

- Avoid high-fat foods such as fried food, chips, cake, and chocolate.
- Eat plenty of carbohydrates throughout the day *(carb loading)*.
- Drink an extra 16 oz (475 mL) of fluid throughout the day.

Immediately before Exercise or Competition

- Consume a high-carbohydrate, low-fat meal 3 – 4 hours prior to exercise or competition.
- Drink 2 – 3 mL of fluid per pound of body weight at least 4 hours before exercise or competition. ** 12 – 18 oz (360 – 540 mL) for a 180 lb person.*
- Drink an additional 7 – 10 oz *(200 – 300 mL)* of fluid 10 – 20 minutes before exercise or competition.

During Exercise or Competition

- Consume a small amount of carbohydrates *(sports drink)* for sustained higher intensity exercise lasting 45 – 75 minutes.
- For long duration activities lasting 1 – 2.5 hours some easy to digest solid carbohydrates can be consumed *(bananas, bread, etc.)* in addition to carbohydrate-containing beverages *(sports drink)*. ***30 – 60 g of carbohydrate is recommended per hour.**
- For anything over 2.5 hours *(ultra-endurance)* 90 g of carbohydrate is recommended per hour. Drink 28 – 40 oz of carbohydrate-containing beverages *(sports drink)* per hour or about 7 – 10 oz *(200 – 300 mL)* of fluid every 15 minutes.
- The main goals are to avoid dehydration and supply enough carbohydrates to avoid mental and muscular fatigue.

After Exercise or Competition

- Consume 200 – 400 calories *(50 – 100 g)* of carbohydrates immediately after exercise and then an additional 200 – 300 calories *(50 – 75 g) within the next several hours.*
- Drink 20 ounces *(600 mL)* of fluid for each pound of body weight lost. Fluid should be consumed within 2 hours post-exercise or competition to replenish hydration to pre-exercise body weight.

Supplements

Dietary supplements are concentrated sources of vitamins, minerals, and energy substrates that are taken to *"supplement"* the nutrients derived from foods.

Ergogenic aids are substances that enhance a person's athletic ability, through either improvement in power or enhanced endurance.

Fitness professionals should not provide guidance or advice in regards to the consumption of supplements by their clients. Supplements are not approved by the Food and Drug Administration (FDA). It's up to the manufacturers to ensure their supplements are safe & effective. The FDA will investigate and take a supplement off the market if found to be unsafe after they become available.

Whey protein: A mixture of globular proteins isolated from whey, the liquid material created as a byproduct of cheese production. **Whey is absorbed by the body quickly.*

Casein: Protein commonly found in mammalian milk. **Casein is absorbed slower by the body.*

Branched-Chain Amino Acids (BCCAs): Essential amino acids, including leucine, isoleucine, and valine, that can be used for energy directly in the muscle and do not have to go to the liver to be broken down during exercise.

Creatine is a compound made in the body, but can also be consumed in the diet, mostly from meat and fish. **Involved in the supply of energy for muscular contraction.*

HMB (beta-hydroxy-beta-methylbutyrate) is a metabolite of the essential amino acid leucine that is synthesized in the human body. Used as a supplement to increase muscle mass and decrease muscle breakdown.

Caffeine has been shown to increase endurance/performance when consumed before exercise. *(5-13 milligrams one hour prior)*

*Note: Excess consumption of any nutrient or supplement does not provide additional benefit. It forces the body to excrete the surplus which uses valuable energy that could be used elsewhere.

Weight Loss

There are many factors involved in successful weight loss. In order to lose weight, an individual must burn more calories than are consumed, creating a calorie deficit. Any successful weight loss strategy must create a caloric deficit by decreasing caloric intake or increasing caloric expenditure through exercise and increasing lean body mass. Fitness professionals cannot prescribe diets but can and should guide clients towards healthy eating habits that create a caloric deficit for those who want to lose weight.

Clients who require meal plans or prescription of a specific diet should be referred to a registered dietitian.

The fitness professional can help clients achieve weight loss by increasing calorie expenditure through exercise.

Clients who are seeking weight loss should perform more complex multi-joint movements at the beginning of the session and incorporate as many multi-joint exercises as possible throughout the session. These types of exercises require the use of large muscle groups which optimize calorie expenditure.

It's just as important to help clients find out *why* they eat in addition to *what* they are eating. Food intake cues can come from social or emotional forces that have nothing to do with hunger. Some individuals use food as a coping mechanism to handle stress, anger, sadness, or loneliness. Food meets nutritional needs of the body, but it cannot fulfill emotional needs. If a client is using food to cope with emotions, advise them to seek the assistance of a mental health professional to help determine the root of their emotional eating and identify new, healthy coping mechanisms.

*Excess consumption of any macronutrient will cause weight gain (Carbs, Fats, Protein).

Empty calories are calories that provide little or no nutrients. The main source of empty calories comes from beverages *(sweetened coffee drinks, sports drinks, sodas, beer, etc.)*

Low-Carb Diets: The rapid weight loss seen with low carbohydrate diets primarily comes from the loss of water.

*Clients looking to increase muscle mass should slightly increase their caloric intake by 300 – 400 calories daily.

*Clients looking to decrease body fat should slightly decrease their caloric intake by 300 – 400 calories daily.

The Female Athlete Triad is a health concern for active females. It involves three distinct conditions:

1) Disordered eating *(poor nutritional behaviors such as anorexia and bulimia)*
2) Amenorrhea *(irregular or absent menstrual periods)*
3) Osteoporosis *(low bone mass and microarchitectural deterioration, which leads to weak bones and risk of fracture)*

Anorexia Nervosa: An eating disorder characterized by low weight, fear of gaining weight, a strong desire to be thin and food restriction. Many people with the disorder still think they are overweight even though they are underweight.

Bulimia Nervosa: An eating disorder that involves binge eating followed by purging.

Binge eating disorder: Characterized by binge eating without subsequent purging episodes.

Domain IV: Legal and Professional Responsibilities

The following areas are covered in this domain:

- Business Basics and Planning
- Training Standards
- Business Plan
- Marketing and Sales
- ACSM Scope of Practice
- ACSM Code of Ethics
- Legal Terms and Laws
- Risk Management Program
- Emergency Procedures
- Injury Prevention Program
- Musculoskeletal Injury Terms

Business Basics and Planning

For success as a self-employed Personal Trainer, business planning, business models, and budgeting are also needed before a business can be started.

Long-term viability relies greatly on the ability of the Personal Trainer to establish and maintain repeat business.

Training Standards

- Personal Trainers must give their clients **undivided attention at all times** during training sessions *(spot exercises, ensure proper technique, answer questions, motivate when necessary, etc.)*
- Begin and end training sessions on time to show professionalism and respect of the client's time and schedule.
- Dress professionally *(in uniform)* or with facility and/or business logo on shirt along with the words *"Trainer"* or *"Personal Trainer."* Attire should look professional and be easily spotted as a Personal Trainer by clients and/or potential clients in the training facility.
- Written documentation should be kept for each workout and client's personal information should be respected and kept private.
- Honesty and scope of practice standards should be emphasized.
- Maintain current personal training certifications, CPR/AED and first aid certifications, and liability insurance if it is not provided by the fitness facility.

If you are unsure of an answer to a client's health or fitness-related question, admit that you don't have the information but will research the topic to provide an answer at the next session or refer them to a medical professional or specialist when necessary. Being honest and upfront with your clients goes a long way and will help build a stronger rapport with them. Admitting that you don't know something but letting your client know you will find out makes you more trustworthy. Anyone who is curious and seeks knowledge understands the more you learn, the more you realize that learning is a lifelong journey. If you pretend to know something that you don't clients will pick-up on it and lose trust in the information you provide to them.

Benefits of Personal Training

- Client achieves results more quickly.
- Reduces the risk of injury to the client.
- Increases the client's motivational levels.
- Provides more focused workout for the client.
- Utilizes the client's time more efficiently.
- Educates the client on physical and psychological benefits of regular exercise.

Business Plan

A business plan should cover all of the following: Mission statement which includes a business vision, business values and a brief description of the business services. The plan should also include demographic and competitor analysis, establish a budget, develop management policies, marketing, sales, and pricing.

Completing a market analysis will help determine perceived value in the marketplace and thus price point.

Six Basic Business Models

- **Sole Proprietorship**: One person owns the business. In the eyes of the law and the IRS, the business and the individual are one in the same.

- **Independent Contractor**: Provides certain services for other individuals or businesses. The primary advantage of this business model is the Personal Trainer's access to health fitness facility's members and equipment.

- **Partnership**: Two or more people who form a business together. Forming a partnership allows pooled financial resources and talents, but each partner can be held liable if another partner fails to meet business-related obligations.

- **Corporation**: A formal business entity subject to laws, regulations and the demands of stockholders. A corporation is a legal entity completely separate from its owners and managers.

- **S Corporation** *(Subchapter Corporation)*: Combines the advantages of sole proprietorship, partnership, and corporation business models. A suitable alternative for small businesses.

- **Limited Liability Company** *(LLC)*: Flexible for small to medium-sized businesses and generally more advantageous than partnerships or S corporations.

Marketing

A market niche represents a client group with similar needs and goals. Assessing the market for potential clients should be based on the following:

- **Client type** *(gender, age, fitness level)*
- **Training needs** *(sport-specific, prenatal fitness, older adult fitness, group training)*
- **Training location** *(in-home, health fitness facility, sport location)*

The following questions should be asked when selecting a niche market:

- What is the potential for income with this market?
- Is this market accessible in my market area?
- Does this market fit well with my training skills and interest?
- Can I feature my knowledge, services, certifications, and skills in such a way to reach this market as my clientele?

*Referrals from satisfied clients are one of the best ways to market personal training services.
*Providing incentives for current clients to refer is a good strategy to get new clients.

Sales

A **sale** is the exchange of goods, services, or property for money. In the case of Personal Training, a sale is simply an agreement between the Personal Trainer or facility and the client.
*Sales should be viewed as a "win-win" situation for both the Personal Trainer and client.

The key to sales success is for the Personal Trainer to **use all available resources**, proactively cultivate warm-market *"suspects"* to convert them into prospects, and finally ask the prospect for a sale.

Generating sales can be accomplished using the following step-by-step process.

- **Step 1**: Making Contact
- **Step 2**: Building Rapport
- **Step 3**: Assessing Need
- **Step 4**: The Tease
- **Step 5**: Presenting a Winning Proposition
- **Step 6**: The Close
- **Step 7**: The Fall-Back
- **Step 8**: Keep in Mind

*For more information on the sales process see Pages 602 – 604 of ACSM's Resources for the Personal Trainer - Fifth Edition.

The ACSM Certified Personal Trainer (CPT) Scope of Practice

Possesses a minimum of a high school diploma, and works with apparently healthy individuals and those with health challenges who are able to exercise independently to enhance the quality of life, improve health-related physical fitness, performance, manage health risk, and promote lasting health behavior change. The CPT conducts basic pre-participation health screening assessments, submaximal cardiovascular exercise tests, and muscular strength/endurance, flexibility, and body composition tests. The CPT facilitates motivation and adherence as well as develops and administers programs designed to enhance muscular strength/endurance, flexibility, cardiorespiratory fitness, body composition, and/or any of the motor skill related components of physical fitness (balance, coordination, power, agility, speed, and reaction time).

- Screen and interview potential clients to determine their readiness for exercise and physical activity. This may involve communicating with the clients' health care team (especially for clients with special needs): Physicians, nurse practitioners, registered dietitians, physical therapist, occupational therapists, and others.
- Perform fitness tests or assessments (as appropriate) on clients to determine their current level of fitness.
- Help clients set realistic goals, modify goals as needed, and provide motivation for adherence to the program.
- Develop exercise regimens and programs (often referred to as an "exercise prescription") for clients to follow and modify programs as necessary based on progression and goals.
- Demonstrate and instruct specific techniques or training programs as well as educate them about exercises that may be contraindicated.
- Supervise or "spot" clients when they are performing exercise movements.
- Maintain records of clients' progress or lack thereof with respect to the exercise prescription.
- Be a knowledgeable resource to answer clients' health and fitness questions accurately.
- Educate clients about health and fitness and encourage them to become independent exercisers (provided they have medical approval to do so).

An ACSM Certified Personal Trainer (CPT) must always operate within their scope of practice and refer clients to other healthcare professionals when necessary. Physicians, physical therapist, registered dietitians and other healthcare specialists are some examples.

These referrals can take place at any point during the trainer-client relationship.
During the initial screening, a training session, or evaluations down the line.

Claims related to violations of scope of practice most frequently occur in the area of supplements.

Code of Ethics

Responsibility to the Public:

- Shall be dedicated to providing competent and legally permissible services within the scope of the knowledge and skills of their respective credential/certification. These services shall be provided with integrity, competence, diligence, and compassion.
- Provide exercise information in a manner that is consistent with evidence-based science and medicine.
- Respect the rights of clients, colleagues, and healthcare professionals and shall safeguard client confidences within the boundaries of the law.
- Information relating to ACSMCP – client relationship is confidential and may not be communicated to a third party not involved in that client's care without the prior written consent of the client or as required by law.
- Truthful about their qualifications and the limitations of their expertise and provide services consistent with their competencies.

Responsibility to the Profession:

- Maintain high professional standards. As such, and ACSMCP should never represent himself or herself, either directly or indirectly, as anything other than ACSMCP unless he or she holds other license/certification that allows him or her to do so.
- Practice within the scope of their job tasks. ACSMCPs will not provide services that are limited by state law to the provision by another health care professional only.
- Must remain in good standing relative to governmental requirements as a condition of continued credentialing.
- ACSMCPs take credit, including authorship, only for work they have actually performed and give credit to the contributions of others as warranted.
- Consistent with the requirements of their certification or registration, ACSMCP's must complete approved, additional educational coursework aimed at maintaining and advancing their knowledge and skills.

ACSM Mission Statement

ACSM promotes and integrates scientific research, education and practical applications of sports medicine and exercise science to maintain and enhance physical performance, fitness, health, and quality of life.

Legal Terms and Laws

Negligence: A failure to conform one's conduct to a generally accepted standard or duty.

Slip-and-fall injuries, equipment issues, free weights, weight machines, cardiovascular machines and claims of sexual harassment are common areas of negligence seen in training settings.
*The four elements that a plaintiff must prove in a negligence claim are duty, breach of duty, proximate cause, and damages.

Informed Consent *(assumption of risk)*: A written statement signed by a client prior to testing or exercise that informs them of testing purposes, process, and all potential risks involved.

Release / Waiver: An agreement by a client before beginning participation, to give up, relinquish, or waive the participant's rights to legal remedy *(damages)* in the event of injury, even when such injury arises as a result of provider negligence.

Tort Law: Body of law that regulates civil wrongdoing.

HIPAA *(Health Insurance Portability & Accountability Act)*: Law that requires health care professionals to have strict policies regarding the safety and security of private records.

FERPA *(Family Educational Rights and Privacy Act)*: Federal privacy law that gives parents certain protections with regard to their children's education records and some control over the disclosure of information from the records.

Copyright Laws: Protect authors and artists original work, writings, and discoveries. One must legally copyright their material & reference any non-original work.

Client confidentiality must also be kept and protected to prevent potential harm to a client's reputation and liability to the personal trainer or business. The personal trainer or business must obtain and store a signed release form before disclosing any personal information about a client. **This includes posting a client's results (before and after photos)*

Risk Management Program

Risk management is a process whereby a service or program is delivered in a manner to fully conform to the most relevant standards of practice, and that uses operational strategies to ensure day-to-day fulfillment, ensure optimum achievement of desired client outcomes, and minimize the risk of harm to clients. The following forms should be kept and maintained to ensure business practices conform to the standards set by professional organizations:

1) Preactivity Screening Form (PAR-Q)
2) Health History Questionnaire
3) Physician's Statement and Medical Clearance Form
4) Fitness Assessment or Evaluation Form
5) Release, Waiver, or Informed Consent
6) Client Progress Notes
7) Incident Reports

A business and/or personal trainer should carry **professional liability insurance** which transfers the risk to the insurance company in the event of an incident or claim by a client. Personal Trainers should take basic precautions such as developing an emergency action plan and an injury prevention plan to help ensure that every training setting is reasonably safe.

Emergency Procedures

All organizations or personal trainers that operate independently must have an emergency action plan in place. **The facility must also have an AED onsite.** Personal Trainers and staff who are responsible for working directly with clients **must have current CPR *(Cardiopulmonary Resuscitation)* and AED *(Automated External Defibrillator)* certifications.** First aid training is also recommended and sometimes required. Failure to abide by the emergency procedures can expose the trainer to legal liability.

Injury Prevention Program

All physical activity involves risk of injury, accidents can and will happen. Death may happen in the extreme case. **Management of these risks is key.**

An area of Tort Law called *"premises liability"* regulates any incidents that result from conditions of the physical setting where training activities occur. Any training setting or premises must have a reasonably safe environment. Exercise equipment service plans along with routine inspections and maintenance of equipment should be performed in order to reduce the potential risk of injury. Providing a safe environment along with the emergency action plan mentioned above will help to mitigate potential liability for incidents that may occur during a training session. **The number one claim against fitness facilities and professionals is for injuries related to falls on the training premises. *Personal Trainers should document any accident or incident immediately, using an incident report form.*

Musculoskeletal Injury Terms

Shin splints: Acute pain in the shin and lower leg caused by prolonged running, typically on hard surfaces.

Sprain: A stretching or tearing of ligaments.

Strain: A stretching or tearing of muscles or tendons.

Bursa: A closed fluid-filled sac or cavity that reduces friction between tissues/joints in the body.

Bursitis: Inflammation of a bursa, typically one in the knee, elbow or shoulder.

Fractures: The breaking of a bone.

Tendonitis: Inflammation of a tendon and/or tendon-muscle attachment.

Patello-femoral pain syndrome: Pain in the front of the knee.

Low back pain: Pain in the lower back resulting from issues with the muscle and/or bones of the lower back.

Plantar fasciitis: Inflammation of the plantar fascia (thick band of tissue) that runs across the bottom of the foot and connects the heel bone to the toes.

The following treatment should be used immediately after musculoskeletal injuries such as sprains, strains, bruises and other injuries: **RICE:** *Rest, Ice, Compression, and Elevation*

Conversions

Fat = 9 calories per gram

Protein = 4 calories per gram

Carbohydrates = 4 calories per gram

Alcohol = 7 calories per gram

3500 kcal (calories) = 1 pound of fat

1 Kg = 2.2 pounds *(pounds ÷ 2.2 = Kg)*

1 MET = 3.5 ml *(VO$_2$ ÷ 3.5 = MET)*

Formulas

Max Heart Rate (MHR): 220 – Age = MHR or 208 – (0.7 x Age) = MHR
e.g. 30 year old would have Max HR of 190 BPM | 220 – 30 = 190 BPM

Heart Rate Reserve (HRR): Max HR – Resting HR = HRR
e.g. 30 year old with resting HR of 60 BPM | 190 - 60 = 130 BPM

Target Heart Rate (THR) = HRR x % Intensity + Resting HR **(Karvonen Formula)**
e.g. 30 year old mentioned above to train at 80% intensity | 130 x 0.80 + 60 = 164 BPM (THR)

Body Mass Index (BMI) = Weight (Kg) ÷ Height (m^2)
e.g. Calculate the BMI of a man who is 6ft tall & weighs 180 pounds
180 ÷ 2.2 = 81.81 Kg | 6ft x 12 = 72 inches | 72 x 2.54 = 182.88 cm | 182.88 ÷ 100 = 1.83 m
| 1.83m^2 = 3.35 | 81.81 ÷ 3.35 = 24.42 BMI

Fat weight (FW) = Body weight (BW) x Body fat (BF) %
e.g. Calculate based on 180 pound body weight & 20% body fat | 180 x 0.20 = 36 lbs. of fat

Lean body weight (LBW) = Body weight (BW) – Fat weight (FW)
e.g. Calculate based on information above | 180 – 36 = 144 lbs. LBW

Desired Body Weight (DBW) = Lean body weight ÷ (100% - Desired body fat %)
e.g. Calculate DBW if the person above wanted to be at 10% body fat | 144 ÷ 0.90 = 160 lbs.

Waist to Hip Ratio (WHR) = Waist circumference ÷ Hip circumference
e.g. calculate based on an individual with a 32-inch waist and 36-inch hip | 32 ÷ 36 = 0.89

VO$_2$ Reserve = VO$_2$ Max - 3.5

Target VO$_2$ = VO$_2$Max - VO$_2$Rest x % of Intensity + VO$_2$Rest (3.5)
The recommended intensity ranges from 0.40 to 0.89

(MET x 3.5 x Body Weight in Kg) ÷ 200 = kcal **(Calories expended per minute formula)**

Acronym and Abbreviation Meanings

ADL: *Activities of Daily Living*

AFI: *American Fitness Index*

AIT: *Aerobic Interval Training*

ANS: *Autonomic Nervous System*

ATP: *Adenosine Triphosphate* (High energy compound required to do mechanical work)

BMI: *Body Mass Index*

BOS: *Base of Support*

CNS: *Central Nervous System*

COG: *Center of Gravity*

CON: *Concentric muscle action*

CRF: *Cardiorespiratory Fitness*

CVD: *Cardiovascular Disease*

DBP: *Diastolic Blood Pressure*

DOMS: *Delayed Onset Muscle Soreness*

DUP: *Daily Undulating Periodization*

ECC: *Eccentric muscle action*

EIM: *Exercise is Medicine*

EPOC: *Excess Post Oxygen Consumption*

FITTE: *Frequency, Intensity, Time, Type, Enjoyment*

FITT-VP: *Frequency, Intensity, Time, Type, Volume, Progression*

GTO: *Golgi Tendon Organ*

HIIT: *High-Intensity Interval Training*

HRR: *Heart Rate Reserve* (Max HR - Resting HR)

ICE: *Institute of Credentialing Excellence*

ISOM: *Isometric muscle action*

JTA: *Job Task Analysis*

Acronym and Abbreviation Meanings

MET: *Metabolic Equivalent (3.5 ml) index of energy expenditure*

PAR-Q: *Physical Activity Readiness Questionnaire*

PCr: *Creatine Phosphate*

PNF: *Proprioceptive Neuromuscular Facilitation*

PNS: *Parasympathetic Nervous System (Rest and Digest / Feed and Breed)*

PNS: *Peripheral Nervous System (Connects the CNS to the limbs and organs)*

RE-AIM: *Reach, Efficacy, Adoption, Implementation, Maintenance*

RHR: *Resting Heart Rate*

RICE: *Rest, Ice, Compression, Elevation*

RMR: *Resting Metabolic Rate*

ROM: *Range of Motion*

RPE: *Rating of Perceived Exertion (6-20 point classic scale / 1-10 point modern scale)*

SAID: *Specific, Adaptations to, Imposed, Demands*

SBP: *Systolic Blood Pressure*

SITS: *Supraspinatus, Infraspinatus, Teres minor, Subscapularis (Rotator Cuff Muscles)*

SMALL Goals: *Self-selected, Measurable, Action-oriented, Linked to your life, Long-term*

SMART Goals: *Specific, Measurable, Attainable, Realistic, Time-Oriented*

SMR: *Self-Myofascial Release*

SNS: *Sympathetic Nervous System (Flight-or-Flight response)*

SSC: *Stretch Shortening Cycle*

THR: *Target Heart Rate*

TTM: *The Transtheoretical Model*

TVA: *Transverse Abdominis*

VRT: *Variable Resistance Training*

WHP: *Worksite Health Promotion*

WHR: *Waist to Hip Ratio*

Additional Resources and Helpful Links

$30 OFF Exam Voucher Link

http://www.fitnessednet.com/cpt-vouchers.html

ACSM Exam Content Outline

https://certification.acsm.org/exam-content-outlines
https://certification.acsm.org/files/file/2017%20ACSM-CPT%20JTA%20(Full)%20final(1).pdf

ACSM Code of Ethics

http://certification.acsm.org/faq28-codeofethics

Exercise is Medicine

https://exerciseismedicine.org/

ACSM Exam Prep Facebook Study Group

https://www.facebook.com/groups/ACSMCPTPrep

Anatomy Websites for Learning Muscle Locations and Actions

https://www.zygotebody.com/
http://www.innerbody.com/image/musfov.html
https://www.getbodysmart.com/ap/muscularsystem/menu/menu.html

Muscles & Motion – Great videos and descriptions of movements that show muscles involved

http://www.muscleandmotion.com/

Poke-a-Muscle – Game to help memorize muscles

http://www.anatomyarcade.com/games/PAM/PAM.html

Preparticipation Physical Activity Screening Guidelines

https://www.acefitness.org/education-and-resources/professional/certified/february-2018/6898/new-preparticipation-guidelines-remove-barriers-to-exercise

http://certification.acsm.org/blog/2018/february/acsms-new-exercise-preparticipation-screening-removing-barriers-to-initiating-exercise

Application of ACSM's Updated Exercise Preparticipation Health Screening *(Video)*

https://certification.acsm.org/blog/2017/august/application-of-acsms-updated-exercise-preparticipation-health-screening-algorithm

Practice Questions

1) Jane is a 53-year-old former smoker who quit 8 months ago. Her mother had a myocardial infarction at age 66. She has a fasting glucose of 100 g and regular blood pressure measurements of 140/95. How many risk factors does Jane have?

    A. 3
    B. 5
    C. 4
    D. 2

2) Restoring proper muscle length-tension relationships are essential to good posture and functional movement patterns. What would be the appropriate action to correct postural kyphosis in a client?

    A. Stretch the upper back (trapezius) and strengthen the chest (pectoralis muscles)
    B. Strengthen the hip flexors and stretch the hip extensors
    C. Strengthen the upper back (trapezius) and stretch the chest (pectoralis muscles)
    D. Stretch the hip flexors and strengthen the hip extensors

3) What position should a pregnant woman avoid after the 3rd trimester?

    A. Supine
    B. Prone
    C. Lateral
    D. Medial

4) In what order does the blood flow through the four heart chambers?

    A. Right Ventricle, Right Atrium, Left Ventricle, Left Atrium
    B. Right Ventricle, Right Atrium, Left Atrium, Left Ventricle
    C. Right Atrium, Right Ventricle, Left Atrium, Left Ventricle
    D. Right Atrium, Right Ventricle, Left Ventricle, Left Atrium

5) What is the function of the tricuspid valve in the heart?

    A. To pump oxygenated blood to the body.
    B. To prevent backflow of blood into the right atrium.
    C. To prevent backflow of blood into the left ventricle.
    D. To pump deoxygenated blood back to the heart.

6) What is ACSM's recommended minimum weekly amount of exercise one should have in minutes?

    A. 300 Minutes
    B. 200 Minutes
    C. 150 Minutes
    D. 250 Minutes

7) What is the recommended amount of daily exercise for the youth?

    A. 30 Minutes of moderate, 30 minutes of vigorous per day
    B. 60 Minutes
    C. 30 Minutes of low intensity
    D. 30 minutes of high intensity

8) What does an isometric muscle contraction describe?

    A. Static hold with no movement in joint.
    B. Same tone throughout movement.
    C. Same speed throughout movement.
    D. None of the above.

9) Which rotator cuff muscle abducts the shoulder joint?

    A. Supraspinatus
    B. Infraspinatus
    C. Teres minor
    D. Subscapular

10) What type of muscle contraction does the quadriceps perform when jogging downhill?

    A. Concentric
    B. Eccentric
    C. Isotonic
    D. Dynamic

11) Which of the following training methods best describes explosive movements that involve jumping?

    A. Circuit
    B. Plyometric
    C. Pyramid
    D. Interval

12) What is the recommended daily protein intake for a 180lb adult non-athlete?

    A. 139 grams
    B. 55 grams
    C. 98 grams
    D. 65 grams

13) Swollen ankles are described by which of the following terms?

    A. Bradycardia
    B. Tachycardia
    C. Bursitis
    D. Edema

14) It is a good idea to keep the following on hand when training a person with diabetes in the event they become hypoglycemic.

    A. Water
    B. Fruit Juice
    C. Nuts
    D. None of the above

15) Which of the following are fat soluble vitamins?

    A. B, C & Niacin
    B. Iron, Zinc & Magnesium
    C. A, D, E & K
    D. Calcium & Phosphorus

16) Which of the following describes the correct sequence of assessments?

   A. Resting HR, BP, Body Composition, Muscular Fitness, Cardiovascular & Flexibility
   B. Resting HR, BP, Body Composition, Cardiovascular, Muscular Fitness & Flexibility
   C. Body Composition, Resting HR, BP, Cardiovascular, Flexibility & Muscular Fitness
   D. Resting HR, BP, Cardiovascular, Muscular Fitness, Flexibility & Body Composition

17) What type of training technique is most likely to cause DOMS?

   A. Forced negatives
   B. Endurance
   C. Isometric
   D. None of the above

18) Training reversibility is best described by which of the following statements?

   A. Gradual progression and physiological adaptations
   B. Reversal of the physiological adaptations gained through exercise
   C. Changing the recommended order of exercises
   D. Performing exercises in reverse fashion

19) What is the recommended order of exercises during a training session?

   A. Large muscle groups (compound multi-joint movements), multi-joint push/pull exercises, single-joint isolated exercises & core.
   B. Large muscle groups, single-joint isolation exercises, multi-joint push/pull & core
   C. Multi-joint push/pull exercises, smaller muscle groups, large muscle groups & core.
   D. Single-joint isolation exercises, large muscle groups, multi-joint push/pull & core.

20) Which of the following terms describes an increase in muscle fiber size?

   A. Atrophy
   B. Hyperplasia
   C. Hypertrophy
   D. Hyperkyphosis

21) Exercising for the enjoyment and long-term health benefits describes which type of motivation?

    A. Social
    B. Extrinsic
    C. Environmental
    D. Intrinsic

22) Which blood pressure measurement is likely to decrease slightly or remain unchanged during exercise?

    A. Systolic blood pressure
    B. Diastolic blood pressure
    C. Resting blood pressure
    D. None of the above

23) What muscle fiber type is best suited for endurance athletes?

    A. Type 2A (intermediate)
    B. Type 1 (slow twitch)
    C. Type 2B (fast twitch)
    D. None of the above

24) John is currently 200 lbs with a body fat percentage of 20%. He would like to reduce his body fat percentage to 14%. What would John's ideal body weight be at the reduced body fat percentage?

    A. 181 lbs
    B. 176 lbs
    C. 190 lbs
    D. 186 lbs

25) Which of the following is NOT a muscle type found in the human body?

    A. Cardiac
    B. Carotid
    C. Smooth
    D. Skeletal

26) A formal business entity that is subject to laws, regulations and the demands of stockholders describes which type of business model?

    A. Sole Proprietorship
    B. Limited Liability Company
    C. Corporation
    D. Partnership

27) The movement of the overhead shoulder press takes place in which plane of motion?

    A. Frontal
    B. Sagittal
    C. Transverse
    D. Horizontal

28) Stretching that involves both stretching and contracting the targeted muscle group describes which type of stretching technique?

    A. Passive
    B. Ballistic
    C. PNF (Proprioceptive Neuromuscular Facilitation)
    D. Dynamic

29) A high-energy compound required to do all mechanical work produced by the human body.

    A. Protein
    B. Creatine Phosphate
    C. Glucose
    D. Adenosine triphosphate

30) Joe is a 35-year-old with a resting heart rate of 50 BPM. What would his target heart rate be if he is looking to train at 80% intensity of his heart rate reserve?

    A. 148
    B. 153
    C. 158
    D. 151

31) Which of the following heart rate sites is not recommended as the first option due to the possibility of reflexive slowing of the heart rate when pressed?

   A. Carotid
   B. Radial
   C. Brachial
   D. None of the above

32) What is the smallest contractile unit of a muscle fiber?

   A. Muscle spindle
   B. Sarcomere
   C. Myosin
   D. Actin

33) The skull, hyoid, vertebral column, sternum & ribs describe which of the following?

   A. Appendicular skeleton
   B. Thoracic skeleton
   C. Axial skeleton
   D. Lumbar skeleton

34) Marie is 30 years old & has a VO_2 Max of 50.5 ml. She is looking to train at 75% of her VO_2 Reserve. What would be her Target VO_2?

   A. 33.25 ml
   B. 38.75 ml
   C. 37.88 ml
   D. 35.75 ml

35) Using Marie's information above calculate what her MET equivalent would be if she decided to increase her training intensity to 85% of VO_2 Reserve.

   A. 11.41 MET
   B. 11.07 MET
   C. 12.41 MET
   D. 12.22 ml

36) Which of the following describes the body of law that regulates civil wrongdoing?

   A. HIPPA
   B. Tort Law
   C. FERPA
   D. Copyright Law

37) There are 24 individual vertebrae in the spine. How many vertebrae make up the lumbar portion of the spine?

   A. 12
   B. 7
   C. 5
   D. 9

38) Using the Transtheoretical Model what stage of change is a person in if they have decided to work with a personal trainer?

   A. Contemplation
   B. Action
   C. Preparation
   D. Pre-contemplation

39) Which of the following correctly describes the SAID principles?

   A. Specific Adaptations to Intense Demands
   B. Specific Adaptations to Imposed Demands
   C. Specific Alterations to Imposed Demands
   D. Specific Alterations to Intense Demands

40) Which of the following is considered the intrinsic pacemaker of the heart?

   A. The Atrioventricular node
   B. The Sinoatrial node
   C. The Atrium node
   D. The Ventricle node

41) A heart rate that is slower than 60 BPM is described by which of the following terms?

   A. Tachycardia
   B. Myocardial
   C. Bradycardia
   D. Claudication

42) If a person is consuming 3,000 calories per day, what is the recommended daily carbohydrate intake in grams per day?

   A. 422.5
   B. 432.5
   C. 487.5
   D. 412.5

43) Daniel is 6ft tall and weighs 180lbs, what is his BMI calculation?

   A. 23.45
   B. 22.42
   C. 25.45
   D. 24.42

44) Intermittent _____ refers to the pain that occurs in a muscle with an inadequate blood supply that is stressed by exercise.

   A. Syncope
   B. Palpitations
   C. Claudication
   D. Contraindications

45) Which term describes a failure to conform one's conduct to a generally accepted standard or duty?

   A. Liability
   B. Negligence
   C. Malpractice
   D. Misconduct

46) Which energy systems do not require oxygen to produce energy?

- E. Metabolic
- F. Anaerobic
- G. Aerobic
- H. Glycolysis

47) Isometric exercises strengthen muscle within ____ degrees of the position held.

- A. 15°
- B. 20°
- C. 10°
- D. 25°

48) What are the six motor skill related components of physical fitness?

- A. Agility, Balance, Coordination, Reaction time, Strength & Power.
- B. Agility, Balance, Coordination, Reaction time, Endurance & Power.
- C. Agility, Balance, Cardiovascular, Reaction time, Strength & Power.
- D. Agility, Balance, Coordination, Reaction time, Speed & Power.

49) What is the optimal spotting position for the personal trainer when a client is performing an overhead dumbbell press?

- A. Behind the client with hands placed on or near their elbows
- B. In front of the client with hands placed on the weight.
- C. Behind the client with hands placed on their wrist below the weight.
- D. Behind the client with hands placed on the weight.

50) Which of the following describes Absolute Contraindication?

A. The benefits of exercise outweigh the risk. Exercise testing can be done only after careful evaluation of the risk/benefit ratio.
B. The risks of exercise testing outweigh the potential benefit. The client should not participate in exercise testing until conditions are stabilized or treated.
C. The risk/benefit of exercise testing is even. Exercise testing can be done only after careful evaluation of the risk/benefit ratio.
D. None of the above

Practice Question Answers

1) **D** / Jane has two risk factors for her fasting glucose of 100 & regular blood pressure measurements of 145/90.

2) **C** / Strengthen the upper back (trapezius) and stretch the chest (pectoralis muscles)

3) **A** / Pregnant women should avoid exercises in the supine position after the 3rd trimester.

4) **C** / Right Atrium, Right Ventricle, Left Atrium, Left Ventricle

5) **B** / The tricuspid valve prevents backflow of blood into the right atrium.

6) **C** / 150 minutes per week minimum

7) **B** / 60 Minutes of exercise per day for the youth

8) **A** / Isometric describes a static hold with no movement in joint.

9) **A** / Supraspinatus: Abducts the glenohumeral (shoulder) joint

10) **B** / Eccentric

11) **B** / Plyometric

12) **D** / 65 grams

13) **D** / Ankle Edema is described as bilateral or unilateral swelling of the ankle(s)

14) **B** / Fruit Juice - A drink or sugar source containing 15 grams of sugar is recommended for people with diabetes who become hypoglycemic (low blood sugar) during exercise.

15) **C** / Vitamins A, D, E & K are fat soluble

16) **C** / Resting HR, BP, Body Composition, Cardiovascular, Muscular Fitness & Flexibility

17) **A** / Forced negatives during the eccentric portion of an exercise have been shown to increase the chance of DOMS.

18) **B** / Reversal of the physiological adaptations gained through exercise

19) **A** / Large muscle groups (compound multi-joint movements), multi-joint push/pull exercises, single-joint isolated exercises & core.

20) **C** / Hypertrophy describes an increase in muscle fiber size.

21) **D** / Intrinsic motivation comes from within (internal) not external sources.

22) **B** / DBP may decrease slightly or remain unchanged with exercise intensity

23) **B** / Type 1 (slow twitch) muscle fibers are best suited for endurance athletes.

24) **D** / 186 lbs | Ideal Body Weight = Lean body mass ÷ [1 - (Desired % body fat ÷ 100)] | 200 x 0.80 = 160 lbs of Lean Body Mass | 160 ÷ [1 – (14 ÷ 100)] | 160 ÷ 0.86 = 186 lbs

25) **B** / Carotid - Cardiac, Smooth & Skeletal are muscle types found in the human body.

26) **C** / Corporation

27) **A** / Frontal

28) **C** / PNF (Proprioceptive Neuromuscular Facilitation)

29) **D** / Adenosine triphosphate

30) **C** / 158 | Target Heart Rate = Max HR - Resting HR x % of Intensity + Resting HR | 220-35 = 185 Max Heart Rate | 185-50 x 0.80 + 50 = 158

31) **A** / Carotid

32) **B** / Sarcomere

33) **C** / Axial skeleton

34) **B** / 38.75 ml | Target VO_2 = VO_2Max - VO_2Rest x % of Intensity + VO_2Rest (3.5) 50.5 - 3.5 x 0.75 + 3.5 = 38.75

35) **C** / 12.41 MET | 50.5 - 3.5 x 0.85 + 3.5 = 43.45 | VO_2 ÷ 3.5 = MET | 43.45 ÷ 3.5 = 12.41

36) **B** / Tort Law

37) **C** / The lumbar portion of the spine is made up of 5 vertebrae

38) **C** / Preparation

39) **B** / Specific Adaptations to Imposed Demands

40) **B** / The Sinoatrial node

41) **C** / Bradycardia

42) **D** / 412.5 grams / The recommended daily carbohydrate intake is 45% - 65% of total calories with the middle range of 55% being recommended for most adults.

43) **D** / 24.42 | Body Mass Index (BMI) = Weight in Kg ÷ Height in m^2 (meters squared) | 180 ÷ 2.2 = 81.81 Kg | 6ft x 12 = 72 inches | 72 x 2.54 = 182.88 (1 inch = 2.54 cm) | 182.88 ÷ 100 = 1.83 (1 Meter = 100 cm) | 1.83^2 = 3.35 | 81.81 ÷ 3.35 = 24.42 BMI

44) **C** / Claudication

45) **B** / Negligence

46) **B** / Anaerobic

47) **A** / 15°

48) **D** / Agility, Balance, Coordination, Reaction time, Speed & Power.

49) **C** / Behind the client with hands placed on their wrist below the weight.

50) **B** / The risks of exercise testing outweigh the potential benefit. The client should not participate in exercise testing until conditions are stabilized or treated.

Thank You!

We want to thank you for choosing our study guide to help prepare for the ACSM CPT Exam. It is truly gratifying to share some insight and help along your journey as a fitness professional. If you found value in the content provided we would appreciate a review expressing your thoughts by following the link below.

   http://www.amazon.com/gp/product-reviews/B01CEZLLA6

~ CPT Exam Prep Team

Visit our website below for additional insights or to message us with any questions you may have while preparing for your exam.

www.cptprep.com
Follow us on social @CPTPrep

Contact via e-mail at info@cptprep.com
Your feedback is welcomed and appreciated!

References

1) ACSM's Resources for the Personal Trainer *(Fifth Edition)*.

Made in the USA
Columbia, SC
23 August 2019